FORGET THE FEAR OF FOOD

The Essential Guide

DR CHRIS FENN

Forget the Fear of Food – The Essential Guide is also available in accessible formats for people with any degree of visual impairment. The large print edition and eBook (with accessibility features enabled) are available from Need2Know. Please let us know if there are any special features you require and we will do our best to accommodate your needs.

First published in Great Britain in 2012 by
Need2Know
Remus House
Coltsfoot Drive
Peterborough
PE2 9BF
Telephone 01733 898103
Fax 01733 313524
www.need2knowbooks.co.uk

Contents

Introduction

Let's face it, there are two types of women: those who are watching their weight, and those who pretend not to be. For a long time now, we have also been told that there are basically two ways to lose weight: on one hand was the safe and effective method – which worked. It involved a slow, steady weight loss and relied on continuous drudgery and self-denial – hardly the happiest time of your life! The other was the opposite. The quick fix of diet pills, milkshakes or some new magic formula based on an extract of South American seaweed that promised to trim you effortlessly. Above all, it was so easy and so quick that you could get on with the rest of your life without even being aware that you were 'on a diet'!

This book is for those who have tried both methods . . . and failed. You may have lost weight, but you are still not happy with yourself. Something is wrong, missing or not quite right with your life but you can't put your finger on it. You will find out not only about food and dieting but also about yourself and how this affects what you eat.

If you look in the mirror every day and say to yourself, 'Wow, you look great. What a lovely face and such a fabulous figure!' this book is *not* for you! Put it down immediately and get on with your life. If you already feel good about yourself, glowing with self-esteem and happy with your body, you won't be able to relate to any of these chapters at all. You cannot understand why the rest of us spend the majority of our adult lives worrying about the shape of our nose, eyes and mouth, or the size of our hips, thighs, tummy and double chin.

Instead, if you see yourself in the worst possible light, despite other people giving you genuine, heartfelt compliments, and you find that you are always aware of your body and regularly point out the bits that wobble, flab, sag, or rub together – this book is for you.

Have you ever tried to lose weight before . . . and failed? No doubt you already have a hefty selection of diet books which promise 'the *easy* way to slim' or 'the *latest* diet discovery – lose weight fast without hunger' . . . which for some reason have not kept that promise. The very fact that some diet plans have a

'There are two types of women: those who are watching their weight, and those who pretend not to be.'

sequel implies that the first one didn't work! They may have left you feeling a failure, worthless and with your self-esteem in tatters. This book is different. It concerns feeling good about yourself, getting your eating habits sorted out – and finding what suits you best, at different stages of your life. It is about taking the guilt out of eating and putting the enjoyment back in.

Have you ever wondered why you put on weight in the first place?

'That's easy,' you might say, 'We get fat because we eat too much.'

This can be true for some people, but the more complex question is to ask *why* do we eat too much? What triggers us to overeat, and what makes us stop eating? For others, it may be the type of foods they are eating – quality, rather than quantity. As you will discover by reading this book, losing weight is not simply a matter of calories in versus calories out. Another important question, which puzzles anyone who has tried to be slim: why does dieting make you fat? This book will give you the answers. Part 1 deals with the problems – why we put on weight. Part 2 will give you the solutions.

'The very fact that some diet plans have a sequel implies that the first one didn't work!'

Obesity – the big problem

There is no doubt that many people in the UK are overweight or obese, and that their health would benefit if they lost weight. For others, dieting has become a preoccupation, a way of life, an obsession – which creates more problems than it has the potential to solve. It is important to identify if you are overweight in your mind, or on the bathroom scales. You need to examine what 'being fat' means to you. At 5ft 4" a woman who weighs 13 stones is fat. But a woman who is 9 stones 5 pounds and wants to be 9 stones is also fat – in her own mind. And if that is where the problem lies, in the mind, then that is where the answers are to be found too.

For many people, diets just don't work because they are based on a quick-fix solution which acts against human metabolism rather than along with it. Chapter 1 will explain why, in the long term, dieting is the problem and not the solution to being a healthy weight.

Fear of food

Many people, when on a diet, are frightened by food – are you? Do you spend your days planning what you are, and are not, going to eat for the next 24 hours? Do you become terrorised by the thought of being asked out to dinner whilst you are 'on a diet'. You are fighting against food every day, with the horror of finally giving in always looming over you. You were doing so well on your diet, but finally you cracked and a forbidden morsel crept past your lips. At first you are almost elated – oh the feeling of relief, that your diet is over and now you can eat anything you want to again. Pretty soon this is replaced with a sense of guilt mixed with weakness and failure; familiar feelings, which come when you have broken yet another diet.

And yet, driven on by the pressure to be slim, we continue to diet. These pressures come from society, and from within. Emotion has an important influence on eating habits – are you an emotional eater? Instead of reaching for the latest slimming sensation, perhaps it is your own attitude to food that has to be changed. Part 2 will show you that there is another way of losing weight and feeling good about yourself. This is based on overcoming a fear of food and boosting your self-esteem. It doesn't involve expensive protein powders, extract of seaweed or a potent cream that promises to melt away the flab. It involves a priceless ingredient – *you*.

Don't be disappointed, or apprehensive, by the fact that *you* can be the driving force behind the *new you*. Think about it. Milkshakes with added vitamins and meal replacement biscuits are a cop out. They are a way of pushing the effort of losing weight onto something other than yourself. The bottom line is that *you* have the power to be whatever you want to be. Slimmer, fitter or simply content with the way you are now.

This book explains how to be the person you want to be. It will give you the principles of healthy eating combined with techniques that you can use to change your attitude to food. After all, it is your belief systems that shape your behaviour. Your mind and the way you think is a powerful tool to changing your eating habits – for life. Society has already brainwashed you into thinking that unless you are a size 10, you might as well give up expecting anything great out of life. This book aims to undo the damage and show how you can develop a much more positive image of yourself; releasing you from the fear of food. Food will no longer be the enemy. The final chapters will explain how to lose weight – if that is what you want. How to lose weight effectively, not by a quick fix, but by learning new eating habits that become part of your way of life, instead of just a temporary diet.

Part 1

The Problems

Chapter One

Starvation or Fasting – The Dieter's Dilemma

Why is it that we can put people into space, split the atom, design life-saving surgical techniques . . . and yet we have a highly profitable diet industry which doesn't work? The figures speak for themselves. There are more diets now than ever before and yet, as a nation, we are getting fatter! Statistics show that 90% of people put back most of the weight they lost within two years of starting their diet. Why is this? What is going on?

Firstly, diets which become popular are usually those which have a gimmick, claim to be effortless and, above all, promise instant and quick results. This attitude fits nicely with our modern society where the essence is speed and the pace of living is fast. We demand instant results, as we race through each day, muttering about having too much to do, in too little time. Text messages allow us to snatch comments with friends or give instructions to children, whilst grabbing a takeaway coffee, on the way to catch the bus, and juggling a million 'to do' thoughts in our head. Instant lottery scratch cards are popular – no need to wait until Saturday to find out if you have won. There is even a 1-minute bedtime story to read to your children. Just cram a whole fairy tale into a few sentences to allow you to go and check your emails, watch TV, and order a pizza to be delivered for supper. The great attraction for most diets is speed; no one wants to spend time losing weight.

The speed of change, and advance in technology has been impressive. You may still have a box of videos or cassette tapes gathering dust in your loft. Renting a DVD is no longer necessary – just download a film onto your computer. Most teenagers today, who enjoy music, will never need to buy a CD. These changes have happened in the last 10 years, and who knows what is coming next? Although technological developments can be applauded, it is this demand for

'Why is it that we can put people into space, split the atom, design life-saving surgical techniques . . . and yet we have a highly profitable diet industry which doesn't work?'

speed and fast pace of living which is out of synch with our metabolism. Our biology has not kept pace with changes in technology. We have a Stone Age metabolism living in the modern world! Think about it. Our ancestors lived in a world which followed the seasons and food was plentiful after a harvest, but scarce at other times of the year. Consequently, nature has designed a system to store excess calories as fat, in times of plenty, to be used when there is a shortage. Women in particular are very good at stashing away any surplus, to prepare for these times of meagre living, and to ensure that the energy demands of pregnancy are covered. However, modern society is very different. Food is available all the time, there are no shortages, and women have many other choices in life other than to focus on the production of the next generation. The modern world has come upon us very quickly, but evolution takes time. Traits that ensure the survival of the species are passed down from generation to generation. We have evolved to be successful in a society which no longer exists.

'We have a Stone Age metabolism living in the modern world!'

Having food available all the time means that we store the excess very easily. This is one reason why so many people are over-fat. Unlike our ancestors, periods of food scarcity no longer exist and there is not the same opportunity to use up our fat stores during the year. However, many people do impose a form of starvation upon themselves; it is called dieting.

If dieting to you means following the latest quick miracle plan and severely limiting your food intake to strange combinations of food (such as grapefruit and boiled eggs; bananas and beetroot), you are on the road to nowhere. These diets do not work. You may lose weight initially but almost certainly this is due largely to a loss of water and, in the long term, muscle rather than fat. This is why it is easy to lose as much as 8 pounds in the first week of dieting. Muscle tissue is heavy because it contains a lot of water and glycogen – the body's carbohydrate store. Compared with our fat stores, the amount of glycogen deposited in our liver and muscles is very small – enough to provide about 600 calories worth of energy (men have more glycogen because they tend to have more muscle, and a larger liver compared with women). Glycogen can be broken down relatively quickly to glucose, which represents an immediate source of energy for the body. If you severely restrict your food intake, your reserve of glycogen is used to provide energy, and the water stored with it is released. At the end of the week you have lost an encouraging amount of weight, but not much fat. This is because your body responds to a shortage of food in rather a strange way. Instead of burning up excess fat to provide the missing calories, it is lean tissue, mainly muscle, which is broken down to provide energy. This is an annoying response to dieting, when your aim is to shift the excess flab, but makes absolute sense in evolutionary and survival terms. Muscle tissue is described as 'metabolically active' because it requires more calories to tick over compared with adipose (fat) tissue. During evolution, if the aim is survival, it makes sense to shed the parts which use up most energy – the metabolically active lean muscle.

Another response to starvation is to turn down the body's metabolic rate to keep energy expenditure down to a minimum. This is another logical adaptation by the body to a shortage of food. It is fine if you are marooned on a desert island and need to survive, but not so great if you are on a diet and live in the modern world surrounded by vast quantities of food. Have you ever seen anyone on hunger strike or a victim of famine rushing around with vitality? If your food intake is severely restricted, you feel tired and lethargic as your metabolic rate declines; you are firing on two cylinders rather than four. Unfortunately, the lean muscle tissue that is lost as a result of dieting tends not to be replaced. Consequently, once you have reached your target weight and return to your previous eating habits, it is easy to pile on the weight – as fat. The end result is that you have changed your body composition. You have lost some muscle tissue and your metabolic rate never really returns to what it was before you went on a diet. What this means is that you now need less food than before – which is why it is so easy to pile on weight again once you go back to your old eating habits.

The lazy way to diet

Diets based on strict portion sizes and ready meals include a daily plan which tells us exactly what to eat, and when. This, for the seasoned dieter who cannot trust themselves to choose food, is very reassuring. There is no risk of temptation because it is all done for you. You know that at 12pm you will have a synthetic strawberry milkshake with a rather floury texture. At 6pm you will eat a small diet bar formulated with a synthetic mix of protein, carbohydrate, fat and a cocktail of vitamins, flavourings and preservatives. If you feel hungry in-between, just reach for the mineral water. These formula, slim-quick type diets sell in their millions, but one of their many drawbacks is that they teach you nothing about how to make a few changes to your eating habits, explore new foods, tastes and textures, to enjoy food and eat well.

Once you have lost weight you can go back to what you were eating before which is probably why you put on weight in the first place. Since you need less food it is easy to overeat, in terms of what your body needs. Yo-yo dieting means that you lose muscle and gain fat with every cycle of dieting. Just think how this affects your body composition, let alone your ego and self-image. Research studies lead by Dr Mike Green at Aston University, Birmingham revealed that dieting caused a lot of mental pressure, stress and anxiety. His studies have shown that dieters have a poor ability to concentrate, their reaction time and short-term memory is also impaired. For anyone who wants to get the most out of life, this is hardly the way to live!

If you break yet another diet, do not expect any sympathy from the slimming food manufacturers. Their message is to keep trying and, more importantly, keep buying . . . all the low-fat products, diet drinks and meal replacements. After all, there is nothing wrong with the diet – it is just your willpower that is at fault.

'Yo-yo dieting means that you lose muscle and gain fat with every cycle of dieting.'

Promises, promises – the diet illusion

We all want to believe that there is a miracle cure, or a magic food, that allows us to eat as much as we want and still shed pounds. The promises that the new diets make are so tempting that we believe them – because we want to believe them. Every time a new diet book or weight loss system comes out, we convince ourselves that this is the answer and religiously follow the rules. However, with every failed cycle of good intentions, dieting, deprivation and lack of willpower comes another slash to our self-image and ego. Crash-dieting makes you fat, but it also shatters your self-esteem and can lead to severe depression.

Picture the scene. It is Friday. Your clothes are tight and there is heaviness in every part of your body. You feel fat, miserable and finally announce . . . 'That's it, on Monday I'm going on a diet.' It's all systems go, but there are two days before then. Time to indulge, knowing that after the weekend your life will revolve around cottage cheese, celery sticks and skimmed milk (which you hate), you owe it to yourself to stock up on a few pleasures before misery sets in. An extra cake, a few biscuits or that special helping of cream are acceptable in view of the impending siege to come. Already your mind knows too well the deprivation that awaits and has given you the okay to overeat. Even before Monday morning dawns you have put on a few extra pounds . . . even thinking about dieting makes you fat.

How can food have so much power over you? How can the same self-destructive diet and binge cycle continue? We deny, refuse, abstain, reject, weaken, fade, give in, eat, devour, binge, and suffer guilt and self-hatred. The apt description 'Yo-yo dieting' simply means that your weight and your self-image go up and down, but no actual progress is made. Magazines are full of stories of women who have lost 250 pounds – about 17 and a half stones! This staggering weight loss is impressive, and you wonder how big they were to start with, until you realise that it is the same 3 stones being lost over and over again. The sad part is that going on a diet and severely restricting your food intake means that, in the long term, you alter your body composition and lower your metabolic rate. With this type of semi-starvation approach, dieting really does make you fat. Why then, if diets don't work, do we diet?

Pressure to be slim – then and now

Our attitude to fatness depends on our culture and where we live. In societies where food is scarce, being fatter than the average person in the tribe or village had several social and biological advantages – especially for women. The average adult female body typically contains a higher proportion of fat compared with that of a man. Pregnancy and lactation impose a huge energy drain on the mother and the extra fat that she had played a vital part in the survival of the foetus when the pregnant woman or her family ran out of food. Fatness in women is a sign and symbol of fertility, health and beauty. A large man is regarded as powerful and as a result there are many rituals associated with feeding up an animal, a child, a bride-to-be, tribal chief or doctor. Our attitude to size in the Western world, where there is plenty of attractive and affordable food, is very different.

'We are brainwashed to believe that slimness equals success.'

Magazines, newspapers and television carry images of the slim and perfectly proportioned. We are brainwashed to believe that slimness equals success. Think of the woman who dances lightly along the beach before tucking into a bowl of Special K. The message everywhere is that good looks and a slim body mean success and happiness. Above all, nothing wobbles.

Feminism tried to release women from the compulsion to diet, claiming that the standards of beauty were dictated by men for their own sexual gratification and that women should be free to choose what they did or did not eat. But feminism is also part of the modern world where the glass ceiling has, theoretically, cracked and both sexes should have equal opportunities at home, in the family and at work. Women can now have it all. However, the successful business woman is portrayed as tall, lean and above all, in control. Slimness, like the company car and expensive, well-tailored suits, are hallmarks of success. Yet to achieve the right look involves a mammoth exercise in self-denial. Women are traditionally the carers, those who nurture and feed. They must buy, cook and serve food to their family or partner but they must not indulge themselves!

Mesmerised by so many images of slender, happy people we are conditioned to believe that this is the only way to be, and yet people come in all shapes and sizes.

Crows and canaries

If you travel across the world there is evidence that traditional populations share certain characteristics. For example, Chinese women tend to be petite with a fine bone structure, whilst African women have rounded buttocks and arms. The fingers and toes of Eskimos are short and thick to cut down the surface area for heat loss. This enables the Eskimos to work outside in the cold, using their fingers, without the need to wear clumsy mittens. Like it or not, you are born with a specific body type and shape that you cannot alter. Your genetic inheritance is therefore an important factor in determining your basic body shape and height. As one larger woman once commented, 'You can't breed crows and get a canary'.

The diet trap

Unfortunately, a lot of self-conscious individuals repeatedly try to transform themselves into a shape that they just are not meant to be. This feeds the diet industry but ruins our self-image and with each failure, makes us feel even more inadequate. If you want to continue with this approach to dieting, go ahead – it's a free country.

Rush out and buy the next diet book or tub of milkshake powder and push yourself through the agonies of deprivation, guilt, denial, and low self-esteem as you fail to maintain your (so-called) target weight – yet again. This approach to losing weight doesn't show you how to change your eating habits and how to uncover the reasons why you have put on weight in the first place.

We live in a fast-paced world, and expect instant results. Low-calorie diets offer a quick fix in the quest to lose weight and conform to the pressure to be slim and happy.

'We live in a fast-paced world, and expect instant results. Low-calorie diets offer a quick fix in the quest to lose weight and conform to the pressure to be slim and happy.'

Summing Up

- The reality is that we are all unique, and forcing your body to be a shape which it can never be is a recipe for disappointment.

- We have a Stone Age metabolism which sees a low-calorie diet as just another famine. The response is to hang on to your body fat, and turn down your metabolism, so that you will survive this 'famine' (or diet) until food is available again.

Chapter Two

Fat People Vs Thin People

Obesity defined – how do you measure it?

Would you describe yourself as definitely fat, going a bit wobbly, or technically obese? Maybe you think you are fat, and just want to lose a few pounds. How we see ourselves is an imprecise science, but research uses underwater weighing and body scanning equipment to accurately measure body composition and categorise obesity. Other methods such as the body mass index (BMI) and the size of your waist are also useful, and less expensive to carry out. BMI is a number, calculated using your height and weight. Simply multiply your weight (in pounds) by 704.5 and divide this by your height (in inches). Divide this number by your height (in inches) again, and this gives your BMI.

If your BMI figure is:

* 19-24.9 – you are a healthy weight.

* 25-29.9 – means you are overweight.

* 30 and over – is the obese category.

This index is useful, but will wrongly classify sports people who have a high body weight, but most of this is muscle. A 16-stone rugby player would have a BMI of over 30, but would clearly not be obese.

Not only is body composition related to fitness and health, but so is the amount of fat stored in different areas of the body. It used to be that total fat was linked with poor health. The more fat in your body, the higher the risk of developing conditions such as heart disease or diabetes. The fat around your

'The more fat in your body, the higher the risk of developing conditions such as heart disease or diabetes.'

middle, known as intra-abdominal fat, is closely linked with certain hormone-related cancers (such as breast cancer), fertility problems, heart disease and diabetes. The exact mechanisms are not fully understood, but it seems that to be apple shaped carries a greater health risk compared with being pear shaped. It makes sense to measure waist circumference as a simple way to add to the statistics of how we are shaping up, year after year.

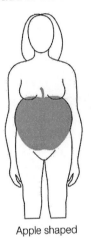
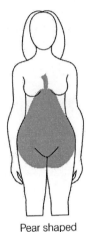

Apple shaped   Pear shaped

Measure your waist, just above your belly button. A healthy waist measurement is less than 40 inches for men, and less than 35 inches for women (together with a BMI of less than 25). Your waist to hip ratio is another simple measurement. Again, measure your waist just above your belly button, and your hips around the widest part of your buttocks. Divide your waist by your hip measurement. A value of less than 0.8 for women and 0.95 for men, is good.

Obesity – how big is the problem?

Take a look around. Notice the people waiting at bus stops, walking down the high street, or taxi drivers and their clients. A lot more people are big. It has become normal to see more of the people who have more person about them. The shape of people has also changed. Young women in particular, have a lot of abdominal fat – 'muffin tops'. There is a reason for this, and all will be revealed later, in the chapter about sugars. Although there are a lot more people carrying a lot of excess fat, obesity is a relatively recent phenomenon. Throughout history there was the usual sprinkling of overweight Roman emperors, and King Henry VIII is well known for his wide girth, but in general, most people were of normal weight for their height. That is until about 50 years ago. Current statistics show that there are more overweight and obese men, women and children compared with normal weight people in most Westernised countries. In America, the figure is just over 74%, Australia is 67%, New Zealand 68% and the UK is not far behind at 61%. This increase in bigger people has happened in the last few decades. There are more oversized individuals walking on the Earth now, than in the whole history of the planet. Think of all those millions in Africa and India who are starving. Well, there are now more overweight and obese people than hungry people on the planet. The worry is that, if this trend continues, the statistics will read that a staggering 90% of today's children will be obese by 2050. New categories are also being introduced. The term 'morbidly obese' cannot cope and a new group, 'super-obese', is needed, as well as the equipment to deal with them. Companies, such as 'Goliath Casket' are suppliers of supersized coffins to cater for the burial of these larger people.

Although there has been a boom in the health and fitness industry, it seems that we will be waddling through the 21st century rather than skipping lithely along, wearing stretch lycra leotards or tracksuits. Clearly, something has gone wrong and a change is long overdue. It seems that many of us have been trying to improve our eating habits – but not succeeding. Why is this?

Why are we fat?

The simple answer would seem to be that we eat too much – but there is a lot more going on. If you factor in a complex society, modern food supply, stressful lives, individual metabolism and genetic factors there is a lot to consider. All of these factors will have some influence on whether you are able to regulate your body weight to within a few ounces year after year, or join those who become obese. If you can understand the reasons why you put on weight in the first place, you are in a powerful position to be able to take control, make some changes, and lose weight. The essence of this book is to help you understand your own path to weight gain, to break free of the dieting industry which only offers you a quick fix solution, and to develop a different attitude to food, that will put you in control of your own eating habits.

Understanding why you have become fat

You may already know the answer to why you have put on weight. However, the dieting industry would want us to believe that it is a simple matter of eating too much, and the key to losing weight is to simply eat less. The surprising

'Although there has been a boom in the health and fitness industry, it seems that we will be waddling through the 21st century rather than skipping lithely along, wearing stretch lycra leotards or tracksuits.'

fact that fat people do not necessarily eat more than thin people means that there is more to the story. Firstly, humans are very well adapted to conserving energy and preserving their fat stores when food is scarce. Many of us are lucky enough to live day to day, in a world of plenty – especially food – so that this ability to survive when food is scarce may seem redundant. However, there are still many communities all over the world where village people are faced with famine and starvation if their staple crop fails. Consequently, nature has designed an efficient system to deal with this and the result is that humans are particularly good at storing fat. We have more fat cells (known as adipocytes), in proportion to our body weight compared with animals which we traditionally regard as blubbery. Pigs, seals, bears and camels all have less fat, relative to their size, than we do. Only hedgehogs and whales have a greater proportion of fat in their bodies!

Can we blame our genes?

'A gene responsible for obesity in mice has been known for many years, and a similar code has been found to exist in humans.'

Think about your parents and compare your body shape and weight with theirs. Obesity tends to run in families, suggesting that genetics has a role to play in its cause. However, it is difficult to separate nature (genetics) from nurture (environment) as your parents not only pass on their genes, but also their eating and lifestyle habits. Studies involving adopted adults have shown that they share a similar body weight to their biological parents. This suggests that, in these cases, the environment and eating habits provided by the adoptive family are not strong enough to overcome the influence of genetic factors.

We have only 26 chromosomes, but thousands of genes. Genes are single units on the chromosomes and contain the coded messages that make us what we are – unique individuals. Each gene is special and is responsible for a specific trait or characteristic such as eye colour, height, body shape and now . . . the latest finding, a tendency to put on weight. A gene responsible for obesity in mice has been known for many years, and a similar code has been found to exist in humans. Rare genetic disorders have been discovered, which have explained why some people are obese. However, research continues to try to find *the* gene which, using gene manipulation techniques, could enable obese people to lose weight permanently.

Even though gene therapy for weight control is still a long way off, it would not benefit everyone. Blaming obesity on your ancestry can only be justified for a very small proportion of the population – only a quarter of very obese individuals. If genetics were a major factor in causing obesity, then each generation would become fatter. Evolution takes time. The reality is that, as a nation, we are getting fatter much faster than can be accounted for by genetics alone.

Your metabolism – fast or slow?

Another explanation for being overweight is having a sluggish metabolism. Metabolic rate is the speed at which your body can burn energy. Thin people claim that they have a high metabolic rate, whilst fat people declare that it takes longer for them to burn off calories because they have a slow metabolism. To test this, Dr Andrew Prentice and his team at the Dunn Nutrition Centre in Cambridge set out to investigate if thin people really do have a fast metabolism burning off excess calories as heat. Groups of both lean and overweight men volunteered for the study and were asked to live for seven months at the Dunn's Nutrition Centre. During part of their stay, they were overfed by more than 50% of their own particular energy needs – that is one and a half times their normal requirement. If an individual needed 2,500 calories per day, he was asked to eat an extra 1,250 calories. The volunteers lived in metabolic chambers, known as whole-body calorimeters – essentially tightly sealed rooms big enough for a bed, washing facilities and an exercise bicycle. They had plenty of windows so that the subjects did not feel completely cut off and, of course, they could speak via a phone to anyone outside. They were under constant supervision, minute by minute, for 24 hours. They couldn't go anywhere and all their food was passed through a small hatch. This meant that the researchers could be absolutely sure of each volunteer's food intake. There was no sneaking out for an extra snack – or not eating the mountain of food that they agreed on for the purposes of the study. Not only was food intake measured, but all waste products and also the amount of energy used up throughout the day. In this study, as expected, the individuals who were overweight to start with, gained weight. But so did the lean group! In spite of claiming that they could eat as much as they wanted, the lean men put on just as much weight as the fat ones (nearly one and a half stones in 42 days). Clearly, the experiment showed that the lean men did not have a fast

'The reality is that, as a nation, we are getting fatter much faster than can be accounted for by genetics alone.'

metabolism which would burn off the excess calories that they were eating. Perhaps the other side of the equation is true; that overweight people have a very slow, thrifty metabolism that makes sure that any extra energy is efficiently stored in the fat cells? Again, volunteers agreed to live for several days in the special whole body calorimeter chamber, and their metabolism was measured. Again, the results from these well-organised studies are surprising. Far from having a slow metabolism, the overweight individuals had higher rates of metabolism compared with thin persons. This means that they also burn calories at a faster rate compared with thin people. In fact overweight people need more calories. They have more muscle tissue (which is metabolically active), and it takes more energy to move a heavier weight compared with a light one.

What is going on? It seems that the human body wants to be neither too thin, nor too fat and has a remarkable ability to adjust its metabolic rate according to circumstances. This adjustment has also been found in people with severe illnesses such as cancer and AIDS. They lose weight very quickly because of their condition, but their metabolic rate is also lowered in an attempt to conserve their energy stores. In the same way, an overweight person needs to use up excess energy and so has a higher metabolic rate. When food is scarce, the body adapts to having less energy coming in by lowering its metabolic rate. The effect of this is to conserve the body's fat stores. As we saw in chapter 1, this energy-sparing manoeuvre is the dieter's dilemma. You may be on a diet and wanting to lose weight, but your body does not know that. As far as it is concerned, a reducing diet equals starvation and it is unable to predict how long the starvation period will last. Its reaction is to adjust the metabolic rate and preserve its fat stores for as long as possible. This makes a lot of sense if you are starving. The ability to alter our metabolism according to the amount of food that we eat is probably the reason why populations throughout history have managed to survive food shortages and famine. However, with supermarkets, fast food restaurants and freezers full of food (all available 24 hours a day), the word 'famine' simply does not apply in most modern societies. On the contrary, there is the very real temptation to eat too much. Snacking and eating on the move has become a feature of our fast-paced society. We try to cram in as much as possible into each day. Something has to go and it is usually the time spent on shopping, the preparation, eating and appreciation of meals. An increasing number of people eat meals, and snack in-between, or simply graze and grab food continually through their busy day. The end result is obesity, even though our metabolism does its best to regulate body fat stores. Metabolic rate is turned down when we eat less (due to starvation or dieting) and is turned up when food is plentiful. And yet we still put on weight! Clearly there are other factors, which apply to how we live now. These modern-day factors seem to have confused our metabolism and led to more people being over-fat – particularly around the middle.

Eat less and exercise more – not the answer!

The simple answer, which most diet manufacturers would want you to believe is that 'we eat too much, and don't take enough exercise'. Strangely, the statistics show that the average person is eating less today than about 30 years ago. In particular, we are following the government's healthy eating advice to cut down on fat and to eat more carbohydrate. Most weight loss programmes centre around the philosophy that you need to eat less, i.e. fewer calories each day. Since fat is a concentrated source of calories (1 gram of fat provides 9 calories, whilst 1 gram of carbohydrate only 4), it would seem logical to cut out as much fat as possible. This has been the main message for healthy eating and weight loss for the past few decades. Food manufacturers have helped us to achieve this pattern by designing and producing a vast range of low-fat versions of cheese, pastry, ice cream, pork pies, chocolate, biscuits, cakes, crisps, and milkshakes. This reduced-fat version is achieved by replacing fat with various fillers, (which are refined carbohydrates), and sugars. A food with less fat, and more carbohydrate, is once again fulfilling the government's healthy eating advice perfectly. Unfortunately it doesn't seem to be working!

Several decades of eating low-fat food has resulted in a nation which is fatter than ever before. This begs the question . . . 'is the low-fat message for healthy eating and weight loss correct?'

Not enough exercise is the other side of the equation. Certainly another big change that has happened over the past 30 years is that we are much less active than we used to be. 'Britain slobs out' and 'Nation of Couched Potatoes' are common headlines used by the tabloid newspapers to describe the average lifestyle in the UK. We just are not as active in our everyday lives as our grandparents were. Our metabolism can cope with a large amount of exercise

'We are following the government's healthy eating advice to cut down on fat and to eat more carbohydrate.'

but it seems that we have forgotten how to use our muscles. According to the latest Thinkbox report, British viewers watch an average of 4 hours 18 minutes of television each day compared with just over 1 hour in the 1960s. There has been a steady increase from 3 hours a day over the past 5 years. Particularly cold winters and greater choice of TV channels could explain the most recent increase. In America, the average home has more TV sets than people. The popular flat screen has made it easy to put a TV almost anywhere. The average American watches 4 hours 35 minutes of television each day. There is a trend in younger adults to watch less, as they spend more hours in front of a computer screen using the Internet or playing electronic games. These involve sophisticated technology and impressive 3D graphics but are designed to stimulate and exercise our brains, but not our bodies. Whatever screen you sit in front of, your muscles are simply being used to shift your bottom from one seat to another. Technology has made life more interesting and convenient but has also taken the natural effort out of daily life and we need to put it back. There are plenty of benefits of regular, moderate, exercise. Firstly, if you choose an activity you enjoy, it makes you feel better. It can be a sociable activity and help boost your self-esteem by being amongst like-minded people. Exercise helps to keep your muscles toned, your body healthy and is a means of stress relief. However, too much exercise at too high an intensity can also add to stress. Competitive types and those who are encouraged to 'go for the burn' by their aerobics instructor can end up, ironically, less healthy compared with someone who never exercises. This is because the stress hormones, cortisol and adrenalin, are released during strenuous exercise, or when you push yourself too hard for your own level of fitness. These hormones, in the long term, can depress the immune system. Ironically, those who try to keep healthy by doing several aerobics classes each week or push themselves to their limit in the latest high-intensity dance workouts, are the ones who suffer regularly from coughs, colds, sore throats and flu.

The latest government recommendation, urges us to build more exercise into our daily routines, as a means of losing weight. However, most overweight people, because they are carrying extra fat stores, will find most exercise difficult and uncomfortable. Jogging and bouncing type aerobics workouts put a strain on hip, knee and ankle joints. Exercise such as walking, cycling, ballroom dancing and swimming are much more suitable forms of exercise which do not bring the risk of muscle and joint injury. However, for anyone wanting to lose weight, these forms of exercise may seem too tame to be effective. The fitness industry is based on the message to do more, faster and for longer, to get fit and lose weight. Treadmills, cross-trainers, circuits and aerobics classes heave with bodies. The air thickens with sweat and the windows steam with the effort of calories being burnt during a 40-minute workout. Why then do we not shed pounds of flab? The answer is that it takes a lot of effort to burn a lot of calories. During strenuous exercise, your body uses carbohydrate (glucose in your blood and glycogen stored in your muscles) to fuel your workout. Once you are finished, you feel hungry. You are likely to put back, in a few minutes, all the calories you have spent the last hour trying to burn off. This is because most processed food contains a lot of refined carbohydrate (usually sugar) and fat. These foods are easy to eat, but easy to overeat. It is more likely that it is the types of foods which we eat which is more important in the war against weight than the amount of exercise we do to burn it off.

Food used to be seasonal and wholesome, nowadays it is plentiful and processed. It is cheapened and adulterated by manufacturers anxious to maximise their profits, regardless of the effect of their food on our health. These products are available for us to take off the supermarket shelves and load onto our plates, or, more likely, to eat straight out of a packet! The effects, of these modern foods on our weight and our health, are the key to understanding how to lose weight – and are discussed in the next chapter.

'Food used to be seasonal and wholesome, nowadays it is plentiful and processed.'

Summing Up

* Obesity is an epidemic, but why are so many more people so overweight?

* Genetic factors do have a role in the cause of obesity, but the rapid increase in obesity since around 1980 cannot be due to genetic factors, as these take time to develop.

* The general healthy eating advice to 'eat less and exercise more' is clearly not working. The food industry has designed low-fat foods which are high in processed carbohydrate.

* The focus on low-fat foods, filled with refined carbohydrates and artificial sweeteners, is good for the profits of the food industry, but is not good for our health.

Chapter Three

If You Are Fat Round the Middle – Here's Why

Walk into a typical superstore and there will be around 35,000 products neatly stacked on the shelves. If you are looking for a biscuit, there will be at least 30 different varieties to choose from. Head for the breakfast cereals and the choice just grows and grows. A recent survey looked at 161 brands to see how many of the extra thickly sugar-coated ones were aimed at children. Worryingly, many of them were, and no doubt there have been a few more popped, crackled and sugar-coated cereals added to the market since the survey. In comparison, the butter section appears to be shrinking, as the latest brands of cholesterol-lowering margarines and low-fat spreads take over. Our food used to be eaten in the area where it was grown. The distance between soil and plate was a short one. Now we live in a complex world with complex food and distribution patterns to go with it.

Over the last half century there have been major changes in agriculture and food production. The basic starchy foods such as potatoes, wheat, barley and oats are now grown as ingredients to be processed rather than eaten in their original form. The starch from potatoes and corn is extracted, extruded, fried and flavoured to produce easy-to-eat snacks which fill the gap in-between meals – or to replace meals altogether. Food scientists have cleverly invented new foods, new flavours and new textures. We now have the luxury of a vast amount of different foods to choose from but, despite the seemingly huge choice, many processed foods are simply rearrangements of the same few ingredients – fat, sugar and/or salt. Another feature of our modern food supply is that the way that food is packaged has changed. Less and less of what we eat is in its original form, especially the carbohydrate in our diet. Potatoes no longer come in their own skin, corn on the cob is rarely seen in this form.

'We now have the luxury of a vast amount of different foods to choose from but, despite the seemingly huge choice, many processed foods are simply rearrangements of the same few ingredients – fat, sugar and/or salt.'

Instead corn starch is extracted and transformed into a refined starch which functions as a filler and thickener to replace good ingredients in low-calorie soups and cheap pasta sauces. Changing the way that nature originally packaged our food, has had a dramatic effects on our health.

Starch

There was a time when a carbohydrate was either a starch or a sugar. Starches were digested and absorbed relatively slowly, whilst sugar got into your bloodstream quickly and was considered instant energy. Starches used to appear on the plate as potatoes, porridge and wholemeal bread. Such foods are also good sources of dietary fibre, B vitamins and some protein. These and other whole, unprocessed foods such as root vegetables, rice, beans, peas and lentils contain 'slow-release' starch. All types of starch consist of thousands of glucose units linked together into large, twisted chains. In this form, the molecules are too large to be absorbed in the intestine, which is why enzymes are needed to digest the starch. Specific enzymes, during the process of digestion, break the links and release the small glucose units, which can then be absorbed into the bloodstream. As the name suggests, slow-release starch is starch that takes time to be broken down by enzymes. This means that the glucose molecules pass gently into the bloodstream. This is how we absorb carbohydrate as nature intended.

Sugars, on the other hand, are small molecules and do not need much digesting and can be absorbed rapidly into the bloodstream.

Food technology has changed all this. We are eating much more starch, but in a processed form. Starch is extracted from cereals or potatoes, processed and distorted from its original form and then added as an ingredient to create new foods. This type of starch is used a lot and can be the main ingredient in some foods. However, once in the body, this processed, cooked starch can be described as 'fast-release' starch. It is metabolised just like sugar – being rapidly digested and absorbed. The result is a sudden surge of glucose into the bloodstream. This is similar to what happens when a large amount of sugar is eaten – more about this later.

Maltodextrin is an example of 'fast-release' starch. It is a highly refined starch. It looks a bit like icing sugar and behaves rather like wallpaper paste in that only a small amount of powder is needed to absorb a large amount of water. When water is added to this fine, white powder, it forms a type of glue. In fact, the substance *is* glue. Each time you lick a stamp or envelope, you are licking maltodextrin! Food manufacturers use this glue as a filler, to bulk out more expensive ingredients. Think of a jar of pasta sauce. This can be made from tomatoes, garlic, onions, herbs and lovely olive oil. This is the wholesome, but relatively expensive, version. Instead you can start with maltodextrin (glue) as the main ingredient, add a few tomatoes, plenty of salt, sugar and flavourings and end up with a jar of gloop which looks much the same as the real thing. However, it is not. Read the list of ingredients to check what is really in the jar you are buying. Maltodextrin (also called modified starch) not only dilutes the good ingredients, but adds to the profitability of these foods. Maltodextrin is used a lot because, as most foods are sold by weight, this is an underhand, but legitimate, way of making large profits from selling H_2O!

Starch is added to so-called 'healthy' foods such as fruit yogurt, cottage cheese, pasta sauces and soups. From a nutritional point of view the added watery starch gel not only behaves like sugar in the body, but also downgrades the food and dilutes the nutritional value.

Sugar

Sugar is another ingredient which can be extracted from its original, natural packaging (sugar beet or sugar cane), and added in huge quantities to foods.

There is no doubt that we love sweet foods – nature has designed it that way. Our first exposure to sweetness is in the womb, bathed by a mildly sweet amniotic fluid. Breast milk, too, is sweet. Nature usually designs things for a reason, and our inbuilt liking to prefer sweet foods is thought to be a hangover from when, as hunter gatherers, we scrabbled around and ate roots and shoots and berries. Some of these would be poisonous but nature has designed a mechanism, based on taste, to let us know if a food was safe to eat. In nature, nothing that is sweet (in its natural form!) is harmful to us. Consequently we learned that sweet foods not only tasted nice, but didn't wreck our guts, or contaminate our blood. Taste was the mechanism to make

'Nature has designed a mechanism, based on taste, to let us know if a food was safe to eat. In nature, nothing that is sweet (in its natural form!) is harmful to us.'

sure that only safe foods were eaten. On the other hand, there are plenty of bitter foods that are poisonous, and these were soon recognised as being unfit to eat, simply by their taste. There are plenty of foods (honey, maple syrup, fruits, berries and dried fruits), which are naturally sweet. These used to be part of our natural food habits contributing to the pleasure of eating by adding sweetness. The ingredients, in their original packaging, also provided a range of other valuable nutrients. Dried fruits are especially good sources of fibre, potassium and beta-carotene; the latter is converted by the body into vitamin A. They are a good nutrient package, as well as containing some nice tasting sugars. These days we can't seem to get enough of the stuff, and the sugar on sale in the shops is made from either beet or cane. The fibre, minerals and all the good stuff is removed, to produce pure sugar. Tate & Lyle is the largest refiner of cane sugar and provides at least half of the sugar that is sold in the shops or to food manufacturers. Mauritius, a volcanic island in the Indian Ocean is the largest exporter of sugar to the EC. The weather – hot, wet summers and cool, dry winters – is perfect for growing sugar cane and almost every field on the island has been turned over to growing the crop. However, apart from the health issues associated with swallowing too much sugar today, the origins of the sugar industry are associated with slavery – and the first human rights issue. Alan Hochschild in his book *Bury the Chains* describes how dedicated individuals devoted their lives to fighting slavery in the British Empire. Whilst the song *Rule Britannia* claims that Britain never will be slaves, black people were considered not to have souls and cruelly used as slaves.

Fast forward through the centuries to today, and the fight is with the food manufacturing industries who are devoted to the production of sugar-rich foods. Children, especially, love sweet things, and the food manufacturers know it! They want to make foods which will be popular, sell in large amounts and make vast profits for the company. They know that the more sugar they use, the more we will like it – and buy it. Consequently, they use enormous quantities of sugar to make new foods, or to sweeten existing foods. Even buns for burgers, peanut butter, baked beans, tomato ketchup, salami (so-called savoury foods), and even cigarettes contain sugar. These are known in the trade as 'value-added' foods because they are based on sugar which is now a cheap ingredient. Sugar, because of its effect on health, has been described as the new nicotine. Get young people hooked on the stuff early, and you have them dependent for life. Research at the Monell Chemical

'Sugar, because of its effect on health, has been described as the new nicotine.'

Sciences Centre in Philidelphia has studied how we develop our early taste preferences and how these can affect our food choices later on in life. Babies have a preference for a sweet taste and this is heightened during growth spurts and through adolescence. One suggestion for this mechanism is that nature steers us towards certain energy-dense foods, which are not only safe to eat, but provide valuable vitamins and minerals needed during growth and development. Unfortunately, nature now has to compete with the baby food manufacturing industry. Although most weaning foods do not contain sugar added directly, many are sweetened with concentrated fruit puree or contain vegetables such as sweet potato. These foods are cooked, put into jars and then heat treated again for sterilisation. These harsh heat treatments alter the texture and break down the potato starch granules to release sugars, in a way that home-cooked food does not. Consequently, jars of vegetable puree taste sweet because of the 12 grams of sugar in a 213ml jar. Fruit-based baby foods have around 35 grams of sugar – the equivalent of 12 sugar cubes – in a 213ml jar. There are plenty of rules and regulations about food – how it should be labelled and what it can, and cannot, contain. It is the job of the Codex Alimentarius Commission to set world standards for foods. At the 2006 Codex meeting, the Thai government, concerned about the levels of sugars in baby foods, suggested that the current standard of a maximum of 30% sugars should be reduced to 10%. It was argued that this reduction would help in the fight against global obesity. This proposed reduction in sugar was blocked by the US and EU. Such is the power of food industries within governments. Driven by profit and not health, the multinational food industry will use clever advertising and techniques to get us to buy more and consume more. One way is to increase portion sizes. The quantity of 'the real thing' in the original Coke bottle, in 1915 was a mere 6.5 ounces (195ml). After the war, once sugar rationing was over in 1955, it became a 10 ounce (300ml) bottle. In 1960 it crept up to 12 ounces (360ml) and in 1992 the 20 ounce size (600ml) was considered normal – that is over a pint of Coke! Only two people know the exact secret, recipe for Coke but what is known is the amount of sugar it contains. Apart from sugar, regular Coke also contains caffeine and salt. The levels of these were increased when 'new Coke' was launched in 1985. The company knew what it was doing. Caffeine is a diuretic and speeds up fluid loss from the body. Salt affects your body fluid composition and makes you thirsty. The end result is that you drink more to quench your thirst, but you are getting an awful lot of sugar along the way.

'Fruit-based baby foods have around 35 grams of sugar – the equivalent of 12 sugar cubes – in a 213ml jar.'

Apart from adding sweetness, sugar is added to processed foods to give them 'texture' or thickness. Tomato ketchup would not have the same gloop, and the sauce would not stick to a baked bean, without the sugar it contains. Not surprisingly, because sugar is a cheap and useful ingredient, food manufacturers are using more of it. Although less packet sugar is being sold, the average sugar intake per person has not changed. The average amount of sugar eaten is 50 kilograms every year, and most of this comes from the sugar added to processed foods. A group of 15-year-old boys were asked to keep a food diary and this revealed that their intake of sugar was around 80 pounds in a year, equivalent to 11,800 sugar cubes. Bearing in mind that food diaries are not a particularly accurate way of measuring food intake, and that studies at the human nutrition unit in Cambridge have shown that people under-report what they actually eat by as much as 34%, those 15-year-old boys are likely to be eating a lot more than the 50 kilograms they confessed to. The food manufactures are adding sugar to sweet, and savoury, foods to make them taste nice, to make them sell and to make the companies a lot of profit – but what is the cost to our ever-increasing waistlines and overall health?

Sugar – pure, white and deadly?

Way back in 1972, a book called *Pure, White and Deadly* was published by John Yudkin. The book warned of the dangers of too much sugar in the diet and the link between sugar intake and diseases such as diabetes, coronary artery disease and tooth decay. We should have heeded his warning and changed the types of foods we eat before the rot set in. Although we are eating fewer total calories today, a larger proportion of those calories come from carbohydrate – especially sugars. The main types of sugars which are added to foods are glucose, sucrose and increasingly fructose – in the form of high fructose corn syrup (HFCS) and more about this later. Nutritionally, all sugars in their pure form are just that . . . sugar. This means that they do not provide any other nutrients; no protein, vitamins, or minerals. John Yudkin's description that sugar is 'deadly' is apt, only today the words 'pernicious', 'addictive' and 'poison' could be added to the description.

We have already seen that even tiny babies love sweetness and many of us enjoy sugary foods. There is nothing wrong with a sweet taste and obtaining pleasure from eating. However the danger with sugar is the concentration in which it is found in processed foods. Sugar in itself is not deadly, but when used in such excessive quantities, often in combination with poor quality fat, it encourages an unhealthy and overwhelmingly fattening pattern of eating. When food manufacturers add sugar to their products they are adding pure calories, often known as 'empty calories'. In effect they are diluting any other nutrients also in the food. In general the more refined and processed a food is, the less nutrition it provides. Many diet foods are highly processed mixtures of various sugars. In trying to follow the Government healthy eating advice, to eat less fat and more carbohydrate, we have become fatter. When food manufacturers remove the fat from a product (soups, sauces, pastry, biscuit, cake, ice cream) to make a low-fat version, they have to replace the fat with something. That something is usually maltodextrin and a cocktail of sugars. This creates a huge variety of processed foods, marketed as low fat and healthy, but which are simply highly concentrated forms of sugar.

There are very few natural foods which are concentrated sources of sugar. Honey is one of these but, apart from by Winnie the Pooh, it is not usually eaten in large amounts. Fructose is the main sugar in honey and in most fruits – which is why fructose is often called 'fruit sugar.' Not all sugars have the same level of sweetness. Fructose is the sweetest sugar and although fruit tastes sweet, the actual amount of fructose in an apple or pear is small, and is diluted by the water content. The end result is that you get enough of a sweet taste, but without much sugar. Lactose, or milk sugar, is at the other end of the sweetness spectrum. It is a very unsweet sugar as it is designed as a first taste for young babies. Although we like the soothing taste, there is a limit to the amount of sugar we can eat before we find it cloying. If milk contained a very sweet sugar, newborn babies, who rely on milk as their very first food, would soon find it so sickly that they would stop drinking it. Nature has specifically designed milk with lactose to give a pleasant, but not overly sweet, taste to encourage the infant to take as much as it needs.

Fresh fruit, some milk and a small amount of honey would give us the sweetness we enjoy, and the level of sugar which nature intended. Instead, we eat, seek out and crave highly-processed, concentrated sugary foods. In terms of our evolution, this is a very new type of food and one which our system is simply not designed to cope with. The rush of sugars into your bloodstream, after eating a sticky bun, a couple of biscuits or gloopy pasta sauce is a real shock to your system – like being slapped in the face with a ten-ton kipper! Apart from making you fat, your brain is

'The rush of sugars into your bloodstream, after eating a sticky bun, a couple of biscuits or gloopy pasta sauce is a real shock to your system – like being slapped in the face with a ten-ton kipper!'

particularly sensitive to too much glucose in your blood. Not surprisingly, sugary foods have been linked with mood changes, low energy, hormonal imbalances and hyperactivity disorders. A recent survey, carried out by nutritionist Patrick Holford, confirmed this. The survey, based on an online questionnaire completed by over 55,000 people in the UK, revealed that the consumption of sugary snacks was by far the best predictor of poor health in all areas of the health categories which were asked about – energy, digestion, immune system, hormonal balance and mental health. There is also plenty of good evidence to show that the average person is very good at converting all this sugar into fat.

Sugar makes you fat

Most people think that energy equals glucose. If you eat lots of sugar, you have lots of energy. This is not true. In fact, too much glucose in your bloodstream can have the opposite effect. A steady, stable amount of glucose in your bloodstream is what your body works well on, and is designed to maintain. You only have about 8 pints of blood circulating through your arteries, veins and capillaries, and your body aims to maintain a steady amount of glucose – equivalent to about three teaspoons – dissolved in it. Too much glucose is harmful as it makes the blood thicker, and your heart has to work harder to pump it around. It also damages the membranes of fine capillaries which take blood to your toes, ears and nose. Ultimately the blood supply to these areas can be cut off, and a sort of gangrene sets in. Since too much glucose in our bloodstream is bad news, we have evolved a system to regulate it within safe limits. If your blood glucose rises too high, the hypothalamus area in your brain (which is sensitive to blood glucose), triggers the release of insulin. This then acts like a key, opening the door to various cells to allow glucose to move out of the bloodstream and bring it back to normal. If the liver or muscle cells take up excess glucose, they can either use it as a source of energy, or convert it to a form of starch, called glycogen, for storage. Fat cells can also take up excess glucose which is ultimately stored as fat. This is how we can get fat by eating concentrated sugary foods. Because the sugar is in a concentrated form, such as a glass of fruit juice, can of Coke, or a couple of biscuits – this does not look like a lot of food. A mere snack in fact, to keep you going in-between meals. However, to your metabolism, this snack is a blast of glucose rushing into your bloodstream – which has to be dealt with, again and again. Regular snacks mean regular onslaughts of glucose. Eventually, muscle and fat cells cannot cope with continually taking in excess glucose from the blood. They throw in the towel and it takes more and more insulin to act as a key to unlock the cells to glucose; these cells become insulin resistant. Your pancreas responds by making more and more insulin. In time, your blood contains too much glucose and too much insulin – both are unhealthy, as the next stage is the development of Type 2 diabetes, with all its associated complications. Blood glucose levels rise dangerously high and a condition known as hyperglycaemia results. The first signs of diabetes are an unquenchable thirst and the passing of abnormal amounts of urine and containing a lot of glucose which the body cannot make use of. The short-term damaging effects of eating sugary and highly processed starchy foods is that you are constantly reaching for more to restore your energy levels, as your blood sugar plummets below normal. The bottom line is that you are eating more than you need. Excess glucose is converted to glycogen; excess glycogen in turn is converted to fat. The epidemic of obesity and diabetes has given rise to a new term, 'Diabesity'.

Many people are insulin resistant, but may not know it, and yet there is one easily recognisable symptom known as 'muffin top' obesity. Depositing excess fat around the waist – apple-shaped obesity – is a sign of insulin resistance. Hormones are incredible molecules and work together to control many areas of metabolism and body processes. When one hormone, such as insulin, is too high it can throw the others out of kilter. Communication between cells is affected and the results can be disastrous – rather like the various instruments in an orchestra being out of synch. Symptoms such as acne and fertility problems can be traced back to insulin resistance – due simply to eating concentrated sugary and refined carbohydrate foods. The modern highly processed foods of today and the high carbohydrate/low-fat healthy eating message is not what our metabolism is designed for. Traditional eating patterns, in many areas of the world, contained a lot more fat and less carbohydrate compared with what we eat today. Traditional carbohydrate foods which were eaten were wholefoods, which were cooked rather than processed, and closely resembled their original state. Too much glucose rushing into the bloodstream was not a problem. So much so that we only have one hormone – insulin – to correct high blood glucose levels, but several hormones whose job it is to bring glucose out of storage and back into the bloodstream. This mechanism is associated with the fight or flight response when the body specifically needs a surge of glucose at a specific time.

'The epidemic of obesity and diabetes has given rise to a new term, "Diabesity".'

Sugar blues

All forms of carbohydrate (sugars and starch) are ultimately broken down to individual glucose units which are absorbed into the blood, causing a rise in blood glucose. However, the extent to which it rises will depend on the type and amount of carbohydrate that is eaten. This is the basis of the Glycaemic Index (GI) and Glycaemic Load (GL) classification of carbohydrate foods. These indices can be useful, but only as a very basic guide to understanding more about how foods affect insulin levels. In practice, the GI system has more limitations than usefulness. Wholefoods containing slow-release starch (found in potatoes, sourdough and good quality wholemeal bread, brown rice, beans, peas, lentils and pasta) or fructose (particularly in its natural form, in fruit) is absorbed gradually. Blood glucose rises gently and insulin is able to make small adjustments to maintain a constant level. Highly processed foods containing refined starch (such as maltodextrin) or simple sugars are very concentrated sources of easily assimilated carbohydrate and are rapidly digested and absorbed. As explained earlier, a sudden rush of glucose enters the blood which in turn produces a surge of insulin in an effort to regulate blood glucose and bring it back to normal. However, the rapid release of insulin removes too much glucose from the bloodstream and the concentration falls too low. This is known as the 'sugar blues' or hypoglycaemia. The symptoms are feeling weak, faint, sweaty, dizzy, exhausted, anxious, moody, irritable, and generally lacking in energy – and of course you are! The fast release processed starch or sugars that you ate, have been rapidly removed from your blood, converted to glycogen and stored in your liver. The brain, being particularly sensitive to a lack of glucose, sends out signals to correct the situation. One effect of these signals is to make you eat something. It works – you believe that you need instant energy . . . and reach for another sugary snack. It is handled in exactly the same way as before, sending your blood glucose into a roller coaster of highs and lows throughout the day. Studies have shown that, when children especially are taken off this roller coaster and blood glucose levels are stable, concentration, learning ability and behaviour are vastly improved. Food manufacturers use sugar in various forms. If used as an ingredient, this must be listed in the table of ingredients on the label. However there are many, legally acceptable, ways of describing sugar. This can be confusing – but, to your metabolism, they all boil down to . . . sugar!

'There are many, legally acceptable, ways of describing sugar. This can be confusing – but, to your metabolism, they all boil down to . . . sugar!'

Sugar by many different names

- Brown, raw or Demerara sugar.
- Cane sugar.
- Caramel.
- Dextrose.
- Evaporated cane juice.
- Fructose.
- Fruit juice concentrate.
- Glucose
- Golden syrup.
- Grape sugar.
- High fructose corn syrup.
- Hydrolysed starch.
- Invert sugar.
- Lactose.
- Malt syrup.
- Maltodextrin.
- Molasses.
- Sucrose.
- Treacle.

Sugar content of breakfast cereals

Breakfast cereals are often considered a healthy start to the day, but some contain more sugar than a jam doughnut or a small slice of gateaux!

Key: 🍬 = 2g sugar

Kellogg's Coco Pops – 15g (per 40g serving)

Kellogg's Crunchy Nut Cornflakes – 14g

Weetabix Mini's Chocolate Crisp – 12g

Kellogg's Frosties – 12g

Vienetta ice cream cake (1 slice) – 12g

Scoop of vanilla ice cream – 10g

Nestle Cheerios – 9g

Jam doughnut – 8g

Kellogg's Special K – 7g

Nestle Shreddies – 6g

McVities chocolate cake (1 slice) 6g

Quick cook, instant porridge – 6g

Kellogg's Rice Krispies – 4g

Traditional Porridge Oats – zero

Two cream-filled biscuits contain 18 grams sugar. The same amount of sugar is found in . . .

- 1 honeydew melon.
- 16 segments of mandarin orange.
- 2 small pears.

- 2 small apples.
- 63 raspberries.
- 6 plums.
- 36 medium strawberries.
- 5 small avocado pears.

Before you recoil and think of the amount of fat (and therefore calories) in an avocado pear – read the 'all calories are not the same' section!

The sweet and sour of fructose

If you are not yet convinced about the dangers of sucrose and glucose, there is another one to consider – high fructose corn syrup (HFCS). Fructose found naturally in fruits, in small quantities, gives them a pleasant taste. In this form, it is absorbed slowly into the bloodstream, does not trigger the release of insulin and so does not produce the same roller coaster highs and lows that most other sugars and refined starches do. However, another feature of our modern diet is the increased use of HFCS in processed foods. Once again, food manufacturers love it. Not only does it add sweetness and palatability, it increases shelf life and texture of a food. Being able to make a food which sits on the supermarket shelf for ages, and still remains 'fresh' after a year is a dream come true, if you are a food scientist. However, the effects of HFCS on metabolism and health are less impressive. Once again the statistics show that we are eating less fat, but more refined sugars – especially HFCS – and getting fatter. This is the preferred sweetener in soft drinks, canned fizzy drinks, fruit juice drinks, breakfast cereals, and all sorts of cakes, doughnuts, ice cream and the toppings that go on them, and even savoury ready meals. Corn syrup is a cheap ingredient, and does amazing things to food (if you are a food scientist!), and food manufacturers are using more and more of it. The use of HFCS increased a whopping 1,000% between 1970 and 1990. Just think how much we are eating now. Statisticians love to look at trends and there is an alarming correlation between the rise in how much HFCS the average person eats, and the rise in fatness. Clearly there is a link, and stand by for a bit of biochemistry to explain how fructose in particular can make you fat.

'The statistics show that we are eating less fat, but more refined sugars – especially HFCS – and getting fatter.'

Corn syrup and high fructose corn syrup, as the name suggests, contains between 40-55% fructose, and the rest is glucose. This sugar ratio is about the same as in honey. However, the concentration of corn syrup used in foods is the problem. This is far higher than that found naturally in fruit and, like other sugars, our bodies are not designed to deal with large amounts of fructose. For thousands of years, the human diet has contained 16-20 grams of fructose, mainly from fruits. Today, the amount of HFCS in a single, 12 ounce (360ml), soft drink is 40 grams. A standard can of fizzy drink is 330 ml, so that is about 8 teaspoons of sugar in a can – which most people drink in one sitting. This level of fructose is easily absorbed and taken to the liver, where it disturbs normal carbohydrate metabolism. Unlike glucose, which is converted first to glycogen and then into fat, fructose is very easily and rapidly made straight to fat. This fat cannot stay in the liver and is poured out, into the bloodstream (and it is not good to have all that fat floating around in your blood) before finally being stored in your fat stores, particularly those around your middle. So, eating a lot of sugar in general, but fructose sugar in particular, will lead you quickly to the being fat but with that abdominal, apple-shaped, muffin top silhouette. Read the labels on food, check the list of ingredients, and if they contain corn syrup, fructose or high fructose corn syrup – avoid these foods. Also avoid the new kid on the block – raw agave nectar or agave syrup. This is often recommended as the new, alternative, natural sweetener. However, agave syrup is even more harmful as it contains 90% fructose. Once again, it is a highly refined and concentrated form of sugar, which is easily absorbed and rapidly converted to fat. Research carried out in 2008 by the University of Texas Southwestern Medical Centre also showed that when fructose is eaten with fatty foods, or shortly before them, the fat that the food contains is more likely to be stored rather than burned.

'The amount of HFCS in a single, 12 ounce (360ml), soft drink is 40 grams. A standard can of fizzy drink is 330 ml, so that is about 8 teaspoons of sugar in a can.'

Sugar and fat – the dangerous combination

To add insult to injury, another thing to notice about many concentrated sugary foods is that they are also high fat foods. It is this combination which is deadly because these foods are extremely palatable. They are very easy to eat – and very easy to overeat! Because they are concentrated foods, it is not difficult to swallow a great deal of sugar from a relatively small portion of food. This sends your blood sugar level soaring, insulin is produced to steer glucose out of the bloodstream and the route to making fat is in full swing.

Sugary foods are fast foods precisely because they do not take long to eat! A chocolate biscuit or an ice cream takes only minutes to devour. Then having consumed it so quickly, it is not long before we are looking around for something else to eat . . . and then something else. Pretty soon, although we haven't eaten very much food in terms of quantity, but because it was so concentrated, we have eaten more than we needed yet again. One of the reasons why so many of us are overweight is not simply because of the amount of food that we eat, but because of the type. Modern processed food is concentrated food, no longer in its original form. Food in its natural state takes much longer to eat. For example, a two-fingered bar of KitKat takes about 20 seconds to eat and will provide 120 calories. The amount of activity needed to burn this off is 15 minutes of moderately energetic step aerobics, or 20 minutes of brisk walking. No wonder people say that they do plenty of exercise but somehow do not lose weight! They may be eating very little food, but if this is concentrated sugary/fatty food they become locked in a never-ending panic/battle to spend around 30 minutes burning off a chocolate bar which has taken 30 seconds to consume. Many diet plans are, wrongly, based on the simple principle that calories in should equal calories out. As will be explained, this is too simplistic and simply does not work. However, by comparing the number of calories from sugary foods with calories from starchy and fatty foods, it is clear that you can eat a lot more of the latter. A small amount of carbohydrate, in the form of resistant or unprocessed starch eaten with other protein or fatty foods is much more satisfying, helps your appetite centre do the job it is designed to do, and helps you ultimately lose weight. For example, the number of calories in a small KitKat can be eaten as two and a half apples or a thick slice of wholemeal bread with butter

1 chocolate custard, Krispie Kreme doughnut (307 calories, 37g refined carbohydrate), is equivalent to:

- 2 medium slices of good quality or home-made, wholemeal, bread with 2 thick slices mature cheddar cheese.

- 2 large bowls of porridge with 25ml single cream on each.

- Wholemeal fruit scone with butter or whipped cream and 1 teaspoon of jam.

- 20 whole Brazil nuts, or 45 whole almonds.

- 1 medium bowlful savoury stir fry brown rice with peppers, onion, garlic and tomatoes.

- 1 medium baked jacket potato with tuna fish or baked bean filling and a green salad (oil and and vinegar dressing).

- 1 portion (8 large) fresh strawberries with 1 carton (125g) natural Greek yogurt.

- 1 large portion of vegetable bake with cheesy topping, 3 florettes of broccoli dressed with olive oil.

Relax – stress makes you fat

It is not only what you eat that is important, but also how you eat. A study in Japan measured the changes in blood glucose, insulin and fat levels in the blood. These were much lower when people were laughing compared with when they were put under stress by giving them mental tests. If you eat whilst you are stressed, or become stressed soon after, the spikes of blood glucose that occur do the same damage as those from eating concentrated sugary foods. Think of the relaxed attitude to lunches that traditional Spanish, French or Italian families have and the siesta which comes afterwards. This could be another reason why Mediterranean eating habits are more healthy compared with highly stressed working lunches and snacks on the run. The hectic pace that most people live at each day has a lot to answer for in terms of its effect on how and what we eat. When we live each day at breakneck speed, few of us taking time to slow down and eat properly. We simply don't have the time to spend on preparing, let alone eating a meal. There are plenty of foods on the supermarket shelves which are concentrated, pre-packed, ready to eat and require very little chewing and digestion. We are busy people, short of time, so thank goodness for all of these foods. If we choose sugary, fatty foods such as cakes, biscuits, savoury snacks, chocolate and ice cream we can actually eat a lot of concentrated sugars and fats (equivalent to around 2,000 calories) in less than 10 minutes. We rush around all day grabbing snacks and fast foods, whenever we have a minute, to keep us going. Chances are that we would have almost satisfied our daily calorie requirement in the form of these snacks alone. Because of the speed at which we can gulp down refined, processed, sugary foods, it is easy to overeat in a short space of time! And yet, at the end of the day we feel justified in tucking into a lot more food because we haven't had 'a proper meal'.

'It is not only what you eat that is important, but also how you eat.'

What a crazy way to live. No wonder many of us find ourselves putting on weight.

44   Need2Know

All calories are not the same!

Many people, who are trying to lose weight, focus on calories. Each day revolves around them. Counting them, trying to avoid them, or giving in and eating them. A calorie is simply a unit of energy, in the same way that a gram or ounce is a unit of weight. The metric equivalent of a calorie is a joule. Your body needs a certain amount of energy (expressed as calories or joules) each day, just to keep alive. The amount of energy associated with keeping your heart pumping, lungs breathing, kidneys filtering and some basic muscle function is known as your resting metabolic rate. Add in some daily activities such as getting out of bed, washing, dressing and walking the dog and your energy (calorie) needs increase. They can go up even further if you have a physically active job or enjoy hillwalking, cross-country skiing, swimming, dancing, playing rugby, squash, tennis or netball and the like. Since we can measure quite accurately how much energy is associated with these activities, it is easy to work out how many calories you would need in a day. The next step may seem logical; you just do the sums. If you know roughly how many calories you need each day, then eating less than this each day would result in weight loss. Your body would need more calories than you are eating, and the difference would be made up from dipping into your fat stores. If the difference was large, the more fat you would use – and you would get thinner quicker. This theory seems sensible and rational, and is the basis of many weight reduction diets, but in reality, your metabolism and the sums are more complex. A common mistake amongst dieters and the weight loss industry is that a calorie is a calorie. This assumes that 100 calories of cola drink is the same as 100 calories of avocado pear and that your body handles these calories – no matter which foods they come from – in the same way. The latest study to dispute this was published in July 2011 in the New England Journal of Medicine. This was a major and lengthy study in which the diets of 120,000 health professionals, including doctors, nurses and dentists, were monitored for up to 20 years. The main conclusion of the study was that the types of foods chosen were more important, in terms of weight management, rather than simply the total number of calories eaten.

'A common mistake amongst dieters and the weight loss industry is that a calorie is a calorie.'

What's wrong with 'diet' foods?

There are plenty of 'diet' and 'light' versions of biscuits, cheese, ice cream and coleslaw. However, it may seem a contradiction, but eating real, good quality foods is the key to losing weight. If your fridge is full of fat-free yogurt, light cream cheese or zero fat salad dressing you are feeding the profits of the food industry rather than nourishing your body. These foods have been designed to cash in on our vulnerability and are cleverly marketed as 'foods' for every dieter's dream. Here is a range of foods guaranteed to take the guilt out of eating. The irony is, that in our quest to avoid calories or fat-filled ingredients, we have lost the meaning of good eating. For example, we are told that butter is bad and that reduced-fat spread, based on vegetable oil, is better. The reality is that many of the spreadable margarines and low-fat alternatives to butter are foul concoctions of water and vegetable fat whipped and stuck together with a cocktail of emulsifiers, gums and thickeners. The mixture doesn't look very nice, and tastes vaguely of plastic and so a squirt of colourings and flavourings are added too. Diet drinks are not any better. They are solutions of coloured water, artificially flavoured and sweetened. Once again, these are cleverly marketed, but common sense would ask 'how can these products, which are so heavily processed and so far removed from the natural state, be good for our health?' The obvious answer is that they are not. They are also part of the problem and not the solution, to weight loss and overall good health.

It may seem crazy, but studies have shown that, rather than helping in your quest to lose weight, diet foods can encourage you to eat more! This is because low-fat and sugar-free foods are unsatisfying, and take the pleasure out of eating. How would you feel after a lunch of reduced-fat cream of mushroom soup, crispbreads with half-fat cheddar cheese and a diet cola? Before long, you are probably reaching for a low-fat yogurt, or fat-free cream cake – just to feel satisfied. Research has shown that, far from helping a dieter on his/her quest to control their intake, some diet foods actually stimulate appetite. Guinea pigs in a study were given fruit yogurt sweetened with real sugar and another with artificial sweeteners. They ate more in the next meal after the sugar-free yogurt to compensate, and by the end of the day had eaten more overall.

The sour facts of artificial sweeteners.

They were heralded as a dieter's dream; sweetness without the calories. Saccharin, discovered way back in 1878, was the first intense sweetener to be approved for use in food. Since then, other chemicals such as cyclamates, acesulfame-K, Sucralose and aspartame (also marketed as Nutrasweet and Canderel) have been found to have a sweet taste many more times that of pure sugar. Nutrasweet for example, is 180 times as sweet as sucrose (white sugar). It is a cheap and very useful ingredient for the food industry. However, plenty of studies have shown that aspartame can break down in the body to toxins which can then contribute to serious nervous system damage. Independent scientists have produced a list of disturbing symptoms in humans including headaches, migraine, tinnitus, mood swings, memory loss, multiple sclerosis and Parkinson's-like symptoms. Nevertheless the food industry convinced the politicians that it was safe to use and aspartame was approved for use in 1981. It is now used in over 5,000 foods including non-diet versions of fizzy drinks, fruit yogurts, breakfast cereals, instant puddings, jams, chocolate and vitamin tablets. It is difficult to avoid, unless you read the label carefully. Alternatively, choose to buy organic food, certified by the UK Soil Association. Aspartame is one of 300 artificial food additives prohibited in organic food. The Soil Association policy is to promote fresh, unprocessed foods which contain natural sugars rather than market aspartame as a healthy way to reduce sugar intake.

Aspartame is made by combining two chemicals – phenylalanine and aspartic acid. All products containing aspartame must carry a health warning because a small, but significant, number of people suffer from PKU, a metabolic disorder in which they cannot tolerate the phenylalanine component. However, even for non-PKU sufferers the aspartame molecule is a source of toxins. It breaks down in the body to release methanol and formaldehyde – two highly toxic substances. It is methanol which is largely responsible for symptoms of nerve and brain damage including dizziness, blurred vision, sickness and possibly brain tumours, All in all, a high price to pay for low-calorie sweetness.

'Plenty of studies have shown that aspartame can break down in the body to toxins which can then contribute to serious nervous system damage.'

Summing Up

- Food technology is a triumph – if you measure its success by the thousands of foods and flavours on the supermarket shelves. But have you noticed how many people are fat around the middle – 'muffin tops'?

- Refined starch and sugars, used in so many processed foods, are rapidly converted to fat in your body, and stored around your middle. Understanding which foods contain these concentrated sugars is a big step to making different food choices.

- All calories are not the same. If you give 2,000 calories of mainly fatty foods to one group, and 2,000 calories of mainly sugary foods to another group . . . it will be the sugary foods group which will get fat.

- Beware of artificial sweeteners. They are unnatural chemicals which your body converts to poisons as it does not know how to use them.

Chapter Four

Appetite and Eating – Are You in Control?

Hunger and gut reactions

How do you know when to stop eating? Why do some people need second helpings when others feel full after much less food? As explained earlier, humans evolved when food was not always available and starvation was a real threat to survival of the species. Those who survived were the ones able to eat the most food, and also use up fat stores sparingly. It is generally agreed that the area of the brain which controls appetite and the drive to eat is the hypothalamus. The exact mechanisms involved in controlling food intake has baffled scientists for decades. Recent research by Dr Alasdair Mackenzie at Aberdeen University suggests that the gut releases many hormones during digestion. These chemicals communicate information to the brain which affect our eating behaviour. Understanding the exact role of these many chemicals will help to explain why some people stop eating far sooner compared with others. The hypothalamus is also triggered by changes in the levels of nutrients such as glucose and fatty acids in our blood, that occur after we have eaten. Biting, chewing and swallowing also send hormonal signals, which help to control food intake, as do stretch receptors in the walls of the stomach. We often feel full and stop eating long before the nutrients from the food have been digested and absorbed into our bloodstream. These various signals work well, but are not the only ones that affect our eating patterns. What we think and believe about food is also a powerful influence. Although there may be physiological signals which tell us when we are hungry or full, there are all sorts of other equally powerful factors which affect what we choose to eat.

'How do you know when to stop eating? Why do some people need second helpings when others feel full after much less food?'

Where does hunger come from?

The purpose of eating is to change the way we feel. When we feel dizzy, light-headed, low in energy or our stomach starts to rumble, these are all signals to encourage us to eat something – and to change the way we feel. Extreme, desperate hunger is a state that not many people in developed countries experience. It is associated with severe starvation, in which we will eat anything. There are plenty of gruesome stories of individuals who, stranded and alone in a rainforest, will eat the maggots crawling from their open, infected wounds. Prisoners of war were victims of starvation, some of whom would resort to chewing the leather of their boots in an effort to get nourishment. For anyone reading this book, the opposite is most likely. Far from being short of food, we have a seemingly infinite variety and amount of food to choose from – and this can cause problems. Supermarkets are stuffed with food – all year round. If we want something different and really tasty, it is there for us to buy. With all this temptation and choice – what makes us eat what we do eat?

If we can understand all the influences that affect our eating habits, we can begin to change them.

Much of what we know about food is learned from an early age. If we were told to 'Eat up your vegetables, and then you can have . . . puddings, ice cream, sweets etc.' this gave us the message that eating healthy foods was necessary, but a chore. We grew up to see certain foods as a compensation for eating the ones we don't like. Cakes, puddings and chocolate are also used for celebration, reward or comfort. Pretty soon as adults, we can decide to indulge in the rewarding foods straight away, helped along by the power of advertising.

Eating with our eyes, ears, nose . . .

We are surrounded by sights, sounds, images and smells that constantly remind us of food. The thought of food, or perhaps just looking at your watch is enough to make you reach for something to eat.

A good tip, often given in weight loss magazines is 'do not shop when you are hungry'. Supermarkets are designed to encourage you to buy more than you intended. The bakery section is warm and pumps out mouth watering aromas of freshly baked bread, to encourage you to buy. And it works! You find yourself reaching for a French baguette, warm and crispy and you can't wait to get home and cover the soft, fluffy centre with butter. Other smells too encourage us to eat. Freshly ground and roasted coffee, the smell of toast or grilled bacon lingering in the air on a Sunday morning all set your gastric juices flowing. Tempting smells, the sight of the packet of biscuits by the kettle, or the half eaten bar of chocolate remind us that food is all around us. The important thing is your response to them.

Food, wonderful food

It has been suggested that the purpose of living is to avoid pain and seek pleasure; eating certainly gives us pleasure. Whenever we eat a food we like, positive feel-good chemicals (endorphins) are sent to the brain. We enjoy this effect, and so keep eating. In time, most foods (no matter how wonderful), will finally lose their appeal, send a negative signal and we will stop eating that particular food. Eventually pleasure is replaced by monotony and we get bored with too much of a good thing. This happens with employees working in biscuit, chocolate or crisp manufacturing factories. New arrivals on the staff think that they have died and gone to heaven when they are told that they can eat as much as they want whilst working. Most do, for the first day or two but by the end of the week are sick of seeing so much of the same brand. However, not all foods have the same monotony value. Fat and sugar make a particularly powerful blend, and foods based on this combination can be eaten in amazingly large amounts – and on a regular basis!

Social eating

When the pleasure of eating is combined with an enjoyable social occasion, such as having a meal out, wanting to prolong the whole event is another reason that might encourage the diners to keep eating. If the restaurant is comfortable, the company amusing and/or romantic and the food is well presented, it is not surprising that we opt for a pudding even though we may

'It has been suggested that the purpose of living is to avoid pain and seek pleasure; eating certainly gives us pleasure.'

otherwise be well past our limit. However, in spite of a large meal, we may not necessarily have overeaten for the day. How many of us, knowing that we will be going out to take part in an event which majors heavily on eating, will curb our intake earlier in the day? This behaviour is related to another condition known as 'internal satiating', which can affect how much we eat. This has nothing to do with the food itself, but with what you believe about the food. If you think that a snack or a certain mixture of foods will fill you up, then it will.

We want what we can't have

Ask anyone who has been on a weight loss diet, and the words 'deprivation', 'denial', 'forbidden' and 'restriction' come to mind. It is human nature to want what we can't have. When we decide which foods are out of bounds during the diet, we all know what effect this has. Somehow our mind focuses on the very foods which we have decided are strictly taboo. When we finally give in and allow ourselves to have them, we go overboard and usually eat far more than we would normally.

'Ask anyone who has been on a weight loss diet, and the words 'deprivation', 'denial', 'forbidden' and 'restriction' come to mind.'

The mechanisms of hunger, eating and not eating are complex. There are physiological signals, produced before and after eating which send messages to your brain. There are also all of the other external sights, sounds and images that constantly remind you about food. On top of that, what you eat is affected by your own thoughts and feelings. The next chapter considers another type of hunger that can also contribute to overeating. It is the hunger that is associated with feelings and emotions, and is much more difficult to satisfy.

Summing Up

- An appetite centre has been identified in the brain. This responds to various signals from your body, after you have eaten – such as the fullness of your stomach or the nutrients in your digestive system.

- Eating is also associated with pleasure and other emotions. These can override the signals given to the appetite centre.

Chapter Five

Your Emotions and Your Food Habits – What's Eating You?

Many people, especially women, are often hungry on a deeper level and suffer from emotional hunger which concerns the needs of the heart and soul. They feel that their life is incomplete and, more importantly, they are not happy within themselves. To the outside world, they may appear content, with a good job and plenty of friends, but their self-esteem is at starvation point. They reach for food and eat to satisfy their emotional hunger. They eat when they are lonely, bored, upset, angry, jealous, depressed, under stress or tired. Does this sound familiar to you? Unlike real hunger, no matter how much food you swallow the feelings don't seem to go away. Instead, you experience another emotion . . . guilt! This is a wasted emotion. It drains your energy, saps your self-esteem and you are trapped in a downward spiral of compulsive eating, fuelled by negative thoughts and the belief that another portion of ice cream will be the answer.

Eating – and overeating – in an attempt to satisfy emotional hunger is one of the main reasons why many people (women in particular) put on weight. Food is a convenient remedy – but only a temporary one. If you can understand your needs and emotions, and how you use food to feed them, it is possible to break free of emotional eating.

'Eating – and overeating – in an attempt to satisfy emotional hunger is one of the main reasons why many people (women in particular) put on weight.'

Food cravings

Animals, such as sheep, horses and laying hens, will deliberately crave – and choose – a particular food. This is because they have a mechanism which detects which nutrients they need, and to select foods which will provide them. Laying hens have an enormous requirement for calcium, and they will crave any food which supplies it. Horses know that they must seek out the salt lick in the corner of the field in order to get the minerals they need. This phenomenon is known as a 'specific appetite' and the closest equivalent in humans is probably the food cravings which many women experience during pregnancy.

The strange mixtures and combinations that an expectant woman would die for may be an indication that her body is lacking in certain nutrients. The powerful drive to eat a particular food may have a very effective mechanism to make sure that it is provided. However, although a craving for strawberries in winter may indicate a need for vitamin C, it seems odd that other foods, which also provide the vitamin (kiwi fruit, oranges, blackcurrants), just won't do. Following the birth of the baby, the mother suffers a rapid fall in the level of certain minerals and vitamins, in particular zinc and vitamin B6. Low levels of this vitamin have been associated with postnatal depression. In an attempt to avoid the 'baby blues', or maybe because they are driven by a definite and quite natural craving, some women reach for a rather unusual source of the missing nutrients – the placenta! Some women swear by it and pack a large freezer bag before they leave for the maternity ward. Placenta cookery is certainly not for the faint-hearted, or vegetarians. 'Take one placenta . . . ' is not the most appealing beginning to a recipe. When it is fried in olive oil, the taste is described as 'gamey' and a bit like liver. The ritual of eating the placenta is not a new phenomenon and makes a lot of nutritional sense, especially in developing countries where the standard of living is not very high. The placenta not only contains trace nutrients but is a rich source of protein, and is highly prized in some communities. Mothers who fear postnatal depression can turn to the old traditions rather than reach for Prozac; placenta eating is encouraged by the National Childbirth Trust.

The foods that non-pregnant individuals crave tend to contain a lot of sugar and fat (such as chocolate and ice cream). This may be due to the particularly wonderful and sensual pleasure that we get whilst eating the food, but it could be more than this. Pleasure hormones, known as endorphins, are released when these foods are eaten. Opium, which is a plant extract, and morphine are drugs which work in a similar way to the endorphins produced naturally by the brain. They can help to control pain but are also thought to influence our mood and eating patterns. It may be that because the endorphins make us feel good, they then create a craving for foods which cause the brain to produce endorphins? It is no surprise that the food industry designs foods which contain both sugar and fat, as these are much more effective in creating endorphins than foods with sugar or fat alone.

Premenstrual syndrome and food cravings

Hormones have a lot to answer for. For some women, food cravings are clearly linked with their monthly cycle. Carbohydrate foods including sweets, biscuits, cake, puddings, white crusty bread and butter are popular at specific times, but top of the list is chocolate. The hormones oestrogen and progesterone do have an effect on our food intake; they inhibit and encourage it respectively. As progesterone levels rise during the second half of the cycle, our appetite is stimulated and our daily energy needs are also increased (by about 20%), at this time. Although energy requirements are increased, ironically tiredness and fatigue are two symptoms of premenstrual syndrome (PMS), which affects millions of women between their teens and their 50s.

PMS is a collection of physical and mental symptoms which can occur at any time after the mid point of the menstrual cycle, and can last from a few days to as long as two weeks out of every month. Over 100 symptoms have been described including anxiety, depression, clumsiness, mood swings, bloating, sweating, headaches and food cravings. The exact causes of PMS are not clear, but nutrient imbalances have some impact. Women suffering from PMS were found to have lower levels of magnesium in their red blood cells compared with healthy, non sufferers. Magnesium is an essential mineral, needed for nerve and muscle function and the body's energy production systems. Magnesium supplements can benefit some women and can help relieve symptoms of depression and low energy. If magnesium and other minerals are so important at this time, it would make sense that food cravings would be for foods to put back the missing nutrients. If this were true, cravings for liver and a large plate of steamed broccoli would be popular rather than sweet, sticky 'junk' foods and chocolate. However, a bar of good quality dark chocolate does contain a reasonable amount of iron and magnesium, but the other highly processed

'Hormones have a lot to answer for. For some women, food cravings are clearly linked with their monthly cycle.'

foods do not. Another effect of fluctuating hormones is a fluctuating blood sugar level. This is a good reason to reach for the biscuit tin, but again other starchy foods (pasta, boiled potatoes, bread and rice), could also have the same effect. Somehow these foods just don't seem to have quite the same appeal!

Social pressures could be another reason for high chocolate consumption amongst women just before a period. There is constant pressure on women today to be successful – at whatever they choose to do. Success is also linked with being slim and in control. Whilst other people, our friends, children, family, boyfriends, partners and husbands tuck into junk food we must remain in control. We restrict our eating, try to choose healthy foods and generally restrain ourselves from enjoying anything as wonderful as a bar of chocolate! But for a few days every month we dig in. This is the time when it is all right to indulge, because we can't help it. We can relax, pig out and not feel guilty because we now have an acceptable excuse – we can blame it on our hormones.

'Stress can be a positive thing and a great motivator . . . but too much can wear us down.'

Stress and eating

Stress can be a positive thing and a great motivator . . . but too much can wear us down. The variety of emotions and hormonal changes that are associated with stress, affect our eating habits. Too little stress can lead to boredom and frustration and the solution to these feelings is often another custard cream biscuit. Too much stress can mean being so busy and caught up in life's problems and anxieties that you only have time to grab a coffee and doughnut between deadlines. Most of us are under a huge amount of stress – often more than we realise. The speed of communication using laptops, twitter feeds and texts has contributed to a lot more stress. For anyone trying to juggle a job with bringing up children, stress can be prolonged and unremitting. The combination of a high stress life with a low-fat/high carb diet causes a shift in the delicate balance of hormones and metabolism, and putting on weight is almost inevitable. This is due to the complex link between insulin, stress hormones and body fat. After years of trying to be 'healthy' and eating a low-fat/high carb diet, based on highly processed starch and sugary foods, your body can become insulin resistant. When this happens, your body converts all those calories from sugars and processed starches into fat – even if you are dieting! Optimum blood sugar and serotonin levels are hard to maintain, which leaves you feeling tired, light-headed and moody. You reach for sugary snacks and caffeine to help you feel better, but this only compounds your insulin resistance, hormonal imbalance . . . and adds to your body fat.

A day in the life of a flight controller at Heathrow is less frantic than that of a woman who must whizz around Tesco before a business meeting and then take a distraught child to the dentist. Eating habits are pushed down the priority list in order to pack more into each day. We grab fast food which can be eaten whilst perched on a desk, kitchen top or car seat and eaten in bursts whilst we do something else. In this way we can at least push food into ourselves whilst preparing a meal for the rest of the family, during work or on our way to taking parcels, pets or children to wherever they need to be. It is not surprising that we put on weight or find it hard to change our eating habits when we are not really aware of what we are eating in the first place. The only thing that we do know is that we are not eating 'properly'.

What's eating you?

Reaching for food as a comfort has its origins in how we were fed as infants. When we cried, it was obvious that something was wrong, but our mother had no way of knowing exactly what it was. Maybe we were upset because we were too hot, too cold, in a room that was too noisy or we were simply thirsty. Whatever the cause, chances are that we were offered food to make things better. If we fell over and grazed a knee, got cold and wet, or had 'been a good girl/boy' we were given something sweet or nice to eat as a comfort or reward. There is nothing wrong with this association, unless it gets out of hand. If we are constantly in need of comfort, we may be doing a lot of comfort eating. Food can also replace, satisfy and act as the nourishment in our lives that is normally provided by other people; love, affection, support, admiration, approval, friendship, encouragement.

The binge cycle

It is hard to define a 'binge'. To some people, it might mean a couple of extra slices of toast, whilst to others a binge can represent several thousand calories worth of food. In general, a binge is taken to imply eating a large amount of food in a short space of time. This is nothing new to us humans. Prehistoric man spent most of his time nibbling on roots and berries until an animal was killed. It was then a case of, 'Hey guys, we just killed a mammoth – let's eat!' There were also periods of not eating, either because they were so full, or because there was no food available. This pattern of gorging and not eating is now repeated, by some of us, thousands of years later. However the reasons for binge eating in modern society (where there is plenty of food available all the time), are much more complex and relate to our emotional hunger rather than simple physical hunger.

Few people could admit that they have never 'binged' at least once in their life. In fact birthdays or Christmas are times when overeating is expected and positively encouraged. This is fine as long as it is part of relaxed enjoyment and the pleasure of eating, and not associated with feeling guilty. The dark side to bingeing means eating a large amount of food uncontrollably in a short space of time. It has nothing to do with true hunger and, once a binge has started, it is difficult to stop. The 'Mastermind' mentality – 'I've started, so I'll finish' – takes over.

'What we cannot have (or do not allow ourselves to have), we want.'

Dieting and feeling deprived is the trigger for bingeing in some people, usually those who are preoccupied with food and are constantly worrying about their weight. These are the 'restrained eaters' who do not allow themselves certain foods and are in a constant state of semi-starvation. The effects of starvation are powerful, especially when it comes to food. What we cannot have (or do not allow ourselves to have), we want. This is the trigger to binge eat, it is almost as if the body knows that it has not had enough food and is trying to catch up. The extent to which people have problems with binge eating tends to reflect how they see themselves, their own self-image, and whether or not they are overweight. The real danger with binge eating is when it develops into the more serious condition of bulimia.

Eating disorders

Bulimia has some features in common with anorexia nervosa, although it is now recognised as a separate illness. Sufferers of both eating disorders have an overwhelming fear of being fat as well as an obsession with food. Bulimics are fixated by the contents of the fridge and regularly stuff themselves with vast quantities of food. They then get rid of this excess, either by vomiting or taking laxatives, but neither method is effective. Vomiting does not empty the stomach completely, and causes damage to the throat and tooth enamel. Laxatives work in the large intestine, beyond the area of the gut where most of the calories and nutrients are absorbed. Getting rid of the food can cause a lot of physical damage to the gut, as a binge can involve eating vast amounts of food. One woman described what she would eat during a typical 2-hour binge: five Crunchie or Snickers bars, a large packet of wine gums, a loaf of bread with butter or peanut butter and two large bowlfuls of cornflakes with milk and sugar. It is significant that many of the foods eaten during a binge are high carbohydrate foods. Some bulimics are physically addicted to their eating habits and claim that the food produces a definite 'high', although this does not last long and is replaced by feelings of guilt and disgust. One explanation is that binge eaters may have low levels of serotonin, a brain chemical which has a calming and soothing effect. Eating a massive amount of carbohydrate alters the balance of nutrients in the blood and leads to the production of serotonin. The binge may just be an extreme way of increasing the levels of this 'feel-good' chemical. On the other hand, bulimia may also stem from the universal social pressures to be slim, from deep-seated anger, or a range of emotions that we are taught to suppress. Many therapists have had a great deal of success in treating bulimics through helping them explore any negative feelings of anger, low self-esteem or helplessness which they are unknowingly taking out on themselves through their self-destructive eating habits.

'It is estimated that 2% of the population suffer from this eating disorder.'

Beating bulimia

It is estimated that 2% of the population suffer from this eating disorder. The first step in beating bulimia, or any eating disorder, is to admit that you have a problem. The next step is to get help and break out of the trap, but seeking help can be a major challenge. For most sufferers, dealing with an eating disorder is an intensely private affair. The good news is that all forms of eating disorders (anorexia, bulimia and binge eating disorder), are recognised conditions and can be successfully treated. The emotional freedom technique (EFT) has helped a high proportion of suffers to take control of their eating habits.

Summing Up

▓ Physical hunger is easy to identify, but emotional hunger is more difficult to interpret. Understanding how your emotions can affect your eating habits can be a crucial aspect in making changes.

▓ Hormones also have a large impact on mood, which can lead to food cravings – especially for chocolate!

▓ Eating disorders are an expression of emotional eating. Several alternative therapies and techniques have been shown to be successful in the treatment of eating disorders.

Part 2

The Solution

Chapter Six

Dieting is the problem, Not the Solution

Crash-dieting and quick fix weight loss plans closely mimic the Stone Age, where food was scarce and the human body was designed to survive famine. Research has shown that when we purposely under-eat, our metabolism is very good at slowing down in order to conserve our fat stores. And yet we follow low-calorie diets in the hope that the less we eat, the quicker we will lose weight. If this were true, the thousands of people who have tried this approach would be thin! Unfortunately, the epidemic of obesity confirms that outdated ideas of calorie counting, and the government's low-fat message for healthy eating advice, is not working. Losing weight has much more to do with eating differently, than it does with eating less. Our metabolism and the gene pool have not changed over the last ten years, but our lifestyle certainly has.

Another major change has been in food itself. Highly processed foods which are concentrated sources of fat and sugar have replaced traditional foods, which are naturally sweet or contain the right type of fats which our bodies can use. Processed foods are 'fast' foods, not only because they are quick and easy to prepare, but also because they are quick to eat – and easy to overeat.

In order to lose weight and maintain a healthy weight over the long term, it is important to understand why you put on weight in the first place. In broad terms, the answer is a combination of:

- The reasons why you eat (driven by your emotions and attitude to eating).
- The type of food that you eat (determined by your lifestyle and knowledge of nutrition).

'Research has shown that when we purposely under-eat, our metabolism is very good at slowing down in order to conserve our fat stores.'

The rest of this book will show you how to understand the reasons why you overeat, and to help you make some changes.

Be honest – and realistic – with yourself

Keeping up with modern life seems to need more than 24 hours each day. We race around at fever pitch and wonder why we have problems. It is important to slow down, appreciate life, and take time to smell the roses. After all, we are human beings, not human doings. Expectations are high – we want to be fulfilled and happy, every day. The reality is that life is full of ups and downs. We seem to have lost the tools to deal with the downs. Instead we wander into the kitchen and reach for food for comfort and consolation. This, as discussed earlier, is a short-term distraction and generates long-term guilt and disappointment in ourselves. So, we resolve to 'get a grip' and mentally list all the foods we can, and cannot, have. Simply screwing your eyes closed and inwardly shouting 'no, no, no!' every time you move towards the biscuit tin is not the solution. Using sheer willpower to deprive yourself of foods, which you use to soothe your emotional state, is doomed to failure. This is because of the conflict between your rational thoughts and your emotional needs. Whilst your sensible, intelligent and rational thoughts are telling you cheese and salad sandwich, your emotions are saying that only double chocolate chip ice-cream will do. Guess which part wins! In this situation, you cannot change by rational thought alone. If you could, you would have done it by now. You need to short-circuit the programme which drives you to eat as a way of dealing with your emotions, and replace it with alternative means of coping. This means that when you are tired, take a break. When you are bored, do something else that is pleasurable apart from eating. Eating nice foods can still be linked with emotions, but not when it is the only response to every emotion. Bringing in new ways to deal with your emotions sounds simple in theory, but is a real challenge in practice. Learning to address and answer your real needs is much more of a challenge than simply reaching for food as an anaesthetic. When you are lonely or fed up, it is far easier to seek some comfort in a bar of chocolate than to reach out to others and perhaps face rejection or not get the response or support you need. When you are angry with your partner, it is often easier to bury your head in the fridge or retreat with a jumbo packet of crisps. These are only temporary solutions; unless you confront the underlying problem, the issues will not go away. A boring job will still be boring, no matter how many cream cakes you eat. A bad relationship will not get any better if you hope that another doughnut will be the solution. Soon food stops being a comfort and becomes the enemy. The food is now in charge of how you express feelings; you are no longer in control of food, it controls you. This is why dieting is the problem, not the solution. By focusing on what you can and cannot eat while on your diet, you are avoiding the real issue – your feelings, and how you respond to them. Simply being on a diet doesn't make things any clearer, or help you face up to the real challenges in your life. All you are doing is adding eating problems to your underlying worries, which with this approach, are not going to change.

The real issue is you and how you respond to the challenges of life. You can make some real and significant changes once you realise that you have the power to take control of your own life, and how you want to live it, simply by changing your own thoughts.

You have a choice. You can remain trapped, living your life as you do now and not making any changes . . . or . . . you can look for new ways to express and deal with feelings and release yourself from depending on food as the solution to everything.

Ask yourself, are you happy? Do you look forward to work, enjoy a good social life, feel relaxed, energised and generally carefree? If the answer is 'not really' then something is not right. Maybe this is the reason why you turn to food, time and time again, and find it so difficult to lose weight. Once you understand how you use food to suffocate your emotions, you have the power to make changes. Making changes is then the next step. There is a valuable saying 'if you always do what you have always done, you will always get what you have always got!' Making a change, however small, will move you on but doing something different can also be a challenge for some people – even when it seems obvious to others!

'Here is Edward Bear, coming downstairs bump, bump, bump on the back of his head behind Christopher Robin. It is, as far as he knows, the only way of coming downstairs, but sometimes he feels that there really must be a better way – if only he could stop bumping and think of it'.

Adapted from *Winnie The Pooh* by A.A. Milne.

'You can make some real and significant changes once you realise that you have the power to take control of your own life.'

Making changes

If your eating habits are based on comfort eating you need to look at the triggers for this emotional eating. This means being honest with yourself and saying 'yes, this is how I am' and 'this is how I use food to cope with life.' Once you have a better understanding of your relationship with food, you know what you are dealing with. You can then take control, and make some changes. Remember that the process of change, from where you are now to being more contented and at peace with yourself and your eating habits, is unique to you. Everyone is different. You may find that making changes comes easily, or realise that you can change but that your pattern is to fall back easily into bad habits. Whatever path you take, it is the discovery and learning about who you are, and being honest with yourself, which is important. This is the long-term approach and a good example of where the journey, not the destination, is the true focus. After all, we go through different stages of life and things are changing all the time. We cannot expect our body image, hormone levels, hair colour, thoughts, attitudes and eating habits to be the same in our 70s as they were in our 20s.

'Once you have a better understanding of your relationship with food, you know what you are dealing with. You can then take control.'

Examine your lifestyle

Your attitude to food – What makes you eat?

Stress

Prehistoric man must have lived in fear of his life. With wild animals waiting and poised to pounce, life must have been stressful. Not much has changed, but the causes of modern-day stress are different. They include being overworked, broke, unemployed, worthless, and the quest to be a good enough wife, mother, partner, employee, friend or lover. Experts agree that a certain amount of stress in life is normal, and even healthy. This type of stress however, should be short-lived. Once you become constantly under stress, this damages your immune system and overall health. It is then a downward spiral as you reach for drugs, alcohol or food to help ease the stress which each day brings.

The important thing is to be able to recognise the symptoms of stress, identify what is causing them, and then do something about it.

Symptoms of stress

Some of the conditions listed below may also be due to other factors, but if you suffer from several at one time, then stress is probably a major factor.

Physical signs

- Constant craving for food, especially when under pressure.
- Always relying on 'comfort' foods (chocolate, biscuits, cakes, sweets).
- Constantly gaining or losing weight.
- Indigestion or heartburn.
- Constipation or diarrhoea.
- Bloated stomach.
- Irritable bowel syndrome (IBS).
- Having trouble getting to sleep and also waking up during the night.
- Feeling nervous, fidgety and biting nails.
- Constantly feeling tired (even when sleeping well).
- Headaches.
- Feeling faint, or dizzy.
- Always getting whatever colds and flu are going around.

Mental signs

- Feeling anxious and trapped.
- Depression, crying or wanting to cry a lot.
- Finding it difficult to concentrate. Not finishing a task properly before rushing on to the next one.
- Feeling out of control.

- Being constantly irritated with other people.

- Not being able to relax, let go and laugh.

- Restlessness.

- Self-consciousness.

- Feeling ignored.

- Loss of interest in other people or other things.

- Feeling isolated and alone, even when with other people.

It is important to realise that many of these are common in people with depression. There are several types of depression including:

- Reactive depression which is triggered by a trauma such as an accident, a serious illness, a family break-up, divorce, or death.

- Postnatal depression. The steep rise and fall of female hormones during pregnancy can result in happiness in some women but depression (the baby blues), in others.

- Seasonal affective disorder (SAD). As the days get shorter around autumn, one person in 200 slides into this type of depression. It is linked with a rise in the hormone melatonin, a hormone which regulates our internal clock. Darkness triggers its production in the body and one effect of the hormone is to make us sleepy. In some people this has a greater effect and causes depression.

It is not surprising that when you are feeling low or under stress, you reach for sweet foods and comfort eating becomes a large part of your life. This could also mean that you put on weight – which only seems to add to your problems. The mistake that most people make at this stage is to go on a diet. They argue that at least if they lose weight, they won't look so bad and will have been able to achieve something. Wrong! In this state you need food. It is acting as a psychological crutch. Take it away and you are bound to fall. Your eating habits will sort themselves out later, your priority is to uncover the causes of your stress.

Life's hard . . . and then you die

This is a rather negative attitude! As far as we know, we only have one life to live, which is a good enough reason to take a more positive approach. Nevertheless, major changes to your life do happen, sometimes out of the blue, and are a definite source of stress. Perhaps one of these events has happened to you recently?

- I left home or moved house.

- I got, or failed to get, a job I was going for.

- A close friend left work or moved away from the area.

- I had an accident

- I was diagnosed as having a serious illness.

- I got married or divorced.

- An intimate relationship began or ended.

- A precious pet, close friend or relative died.

- An important source of income was reduced or ended.

- I won ten million pounds on the National Lottery!

Any one of these events can radically alter your view of life and/or your lifestyle. Chances are that your eating habits changed as well. Some people totally lose their appetite after a traumatic event. This is because whatever has happened (an accident, serious illness, losing your job or a death of a friend or member of your family), has totally taken over your life. You cannot think, or function as you did before. You may be able to carry on some sort of routine, but it is as though you are on automatic pilot. You are numb to the outside world and your eyes stare with a rather glazed expression. Your heartbeat rises above normal, you may become sweaty and then shivery, you become tense and your breathing becomes faster and shallower compared with normal. Your salivary glands don't function properly and your mouth becomes dry. Your digestive system shuts down and preparing or eating food is the last thing you find yourself thinking about. This is not surprising because your blood is primed with plenty of energy. The release of adrenalin, one of the stress hormones, is the reason for this. One effect of adrenalin is to make the blood stickier which

'As far as we know, we only have one life to live, which is a good enough reason to take a more positive approach.'

means that it will clot faster (it would have helped wound healing in our Stone Age ancestors). Adrenalin also promotes the breakdown of glycogen, stored in your liver and muscles, to release glucose into the bloodstream. Fat stores are also triggered to release fatty acids, and provide fuel for the body. The end result is that the body is primed with energy and ready for action. However, these days there is nothing to attack or run from and the best release for this energy is to pace up and down or thump a pillow. Constant stress means that our bloodstream remains flooded with adrenalin, glucose and fatty acids. In the long term, this can lead to adrenal burn out and severe fatigue.

Alternatively, prolonged stress can result in weight gain. There is a powerful link between stress and body fat. Another stress hormone, cortisol, blocks weight loss. The body interprets long-term stress as a famine and tries to hang on to fat stores – which it does very effectively, regardless of how much food you are eating. There is a complex interplay between appetite, stress hormones and body fat.

'Unresolved emotional issues are often a source of stress and contribute to poor eating habits.'

Our daily stress

Unresolved emotional issues are often a source of stress and contribute to poor eating habits. You feel irritable, tense, tired and generally 'wound up'. You eat junk food for some comfort, but you put on weight. This makes you feel bad and adds to your stress. You eat junk food . . . it is a vicious cycle. You need to break the cycle and identify the major causes of your stress. Stressors can be physical (too much noise, too hot, too cold) as well as emotional.

Study the events listed opposite and consider how each relates to your situation. Give each an emotional impact score according to if, or how, they have affected you in the last 12 months.

Give 1 for a low impact and up to 10 for a major impact. Only score those events that have occurred. For example, if your job demands more time than you want to give it and you feel that this is the cause of a lot of stress to you, then give a high score of 7 or 8. Ignore those items that did not occur, or do not apply to you.

Event	Score
My paid work load is excessive	
My work schedule creates problems	
I haven't enough time that I can call my own – 'me time'.	
My outside relationships conflict with work.	
I question the value of home life	
I question the value I get from work life.	
My budget is too restrictive.	
My friend(s) or family tend to rule my life.	
I have ongoing problems with one or more of my work colleagues or neighbours.	
I feel self-conscious about myself (e.g. weight, appearance, social skills).	

The process of thinking about these areas of your life, not necessarily your absolute score, will help you to identify the possible sources of stress. Once you know what is causing the stress, you have the power to change things.

Do you need a 26-hour day?

Many women are stressed because they are time pressured. Men are very good at focusing on one thing (usually their work or career). They leave the rest of life's trivia (shopping, cooking, laundry, filling the freezer, ironing) to somebody else. In contrast, women try to do it all, all at once. They weave their lives around their jobs, work, children, family, partners and social life. This leaves very little time for themselves. Time to slow down, to stop . . . and relax. It is not everlasting youth or wrinkle cream that many women hunger for, but free time! If you have scored highly on numbers 1, 2 and 3 of your emotional impact list, then time management and lack of time is a major source of stress for you. Look back at the symptoms of stress and if you suffer from tension headaches, feel constantly tired and find yourself eating fast/junk food because you don't have time to grab anything else . . . the answer is that you need to make time for yourself and learn how to relax. There are plenty of opportunities to de-stress and relax. This can be a challenge and you may need to kick-start the process with a regular massage or reflexology session, book yourself into a spa hotel for a weekend, or on a self-development holiday. These can give you the time and space to recover and think about how to change the lifestyle that is causing the stress! A suggested list of these holidays is given in the help list.

Another effective therapy for stress is cognitive behavioural therapy (CBT). This approach allows you to talk about your lifestyle with a trained expert. They will help you understand that it is not the situation itself, but how you deal with it that can ease the stress. You will learn how to reassess how you respond to stress, and to develop tools and techniques to cope in a different way. Your ability to change things, to take control of your life comes from your own self-esteem and your own self-image. Building confidence and self-image to make changes to the way you live your life is the first step. Once you can do this, changes to your eating habits will follow – and you may discover that you don't even have to resort to going on a 'diet'!

Summing Up

- Simply using willpower to resist eating foods which you think are unhealthy does not work. Understanding your attitude to life, and realising that you have the power to take control of your eating habits is a much more successful approach. Food then becomes something which you enjoy, rather than fear. You move from being a victim of your own eating habits, to being in control of them.

- Take stock of your stress levels, and identify which aspects of your life are causing most stress and affecting your eating habits.

- You may uncover some major stressors in your life, which you had not realised, that are the root cause of your poor eating habits.

Chapter Seven

Step Up Your Self-Esteem

An important aspect of maintaining a comfortable weight is to feel good about yourself. Never mind what other people think of you, it is how *you* feel about *yourself* that counts.

Other people may tell you how wonderful you are, but you never seem to believe them! Giving someone a compliment is rather like handing them a present. It is considered rude to refuse a gift, and yet we do it all the time with compliments!

It is well known that your thoughts have a powerful effect on how you feel, and how you behave. Negative thoughts can drag you down and affect your self-esteem. This is the point at which you become a member of the 'If Only' club.

If only I were slim, then I would . . . go out and do things, have more friends, enjoy going shopping, be happier . . . and so on.

This way of thinking only traps you into a vicious circle of waiting until you have lost weight before you can do all the things you want to, but you cannot lose weight because you are so depressed!

To break free, you need to change the way you think about yourself, and find ways to build your self-esteem. This is usually a challenge for most people, but there is plenty of expert advice and different approaches to changing the way you think, your belief system and how you see the world . . . and yourself. The trick is to find the method which suits you. Byron Katie has developed a very effective method called 'The Work' which has helped thousands of people to be happy. Dr David Hamilton has studied the positive impact of compassion and kindness on the mind. Another approach is neuro-linguistic programming

'Never mind what other people think of you, it is how you feel about yourself that counts.'

(NLP). How we think is influenced by the words we use, and the principles of NLP include changing your vocabulary. Think about the words that you use to describe yourself? Aim to change these from those in the left-hand column, to those on the right.

Feelings Vocabulary

Negative	Positive
Pessimistic	Happy
Scared	Carefree
Vulnerable	Secure
Miserable	Delighted
Lost	Confident
Resentful	Trusting
Suspicious	Enthusiastic
Gloomy	Contented
Helpless	Powerful
Depressed	Determined
Apprehensive	Impulsive
Cautious	Elated
Exasperated	Fulfilled
Bored	Lively
Envious	Extravagant
Irritated	Pleased
Furious	Fabulous
Problematical	Adventurous

It is not only what you say, but how you say it.

- Your posture – do you slouch . . . or stand tall?

- Your expression – do you smile . . . or look grim?

- Your mannerisms – are you relaxed . . . or do you fidget?

All of these can signal a lot about you to others. Anyone can buy stylish clothes, but do you wear them with style and confidence. It is often said that if you dress well, you notice the clothes, if you dress with confidence you notice the woman! Confidence comes from within. That niggling voice inside you (often described as your 'self talk') can drag you down with negative thoughts, or be the source of your inner power. Positive thinking is a powerful tool to help boost your self-esteem. This can be a challenge in a world full of bad news and negative people, but here are some things to practise.

- Be grateful – there is always someone worse off than you.

- Look for the silver lining and try to see the benefit in everything. It is so easy to focus on disaster and trauma, and there is plenty in the world, but aim to be creative and come up with a silver lining (however flimsy it may be).

- Let go of comparisons. When we compare ourselves to others, this is often a source of disappointment and sadness, which only fuels a negative view. Be yourself and do not judge others.

- Celebrate the success of others, without falling into competition.

- Avoid being a victim when life does not go your way. Shift your thinking from 'why is this happening to me?' to 'what is the lesson here for me?' Try to look for the lessons in life, and not the loss.

- Be happy. Research shows that happiness and laughter release feel-good chemicals in the brain. It's official, smiling is good for health.

'Confidence comes from within.'

Smiling

'Smiling is infectious, you catch it like the flu. When someone smiled at me today, I started smiling too.'

'I walked around the corner, and someone saw me grin. When he smiled, I realised I had passed it onto him.'

'I thought about the smile, and then realised its worth – a single smile, like mine, could travel round the earth.'

So if you find a smile begin, don't leave it undetected; start an epidemic quick, and get the world infected.'

Anon.

Perhaps all that you need to know about life can be learned from your teddy

bear . . .

> **'If you find a smile begin, don't leave it undetected; start an epidemic quick, and get the world infected.'**
>
> Anon

'Hugs are better than chocolate
There's no such thing as too many kisses
One good cuddle can change a grumpy day
Love is supposed to wear out your fur a little
It's okay to let your inside stuffing show now and then
Listening is as important as talking
Someone's got to keep their eyes open all the time
It's never too late to have a happy childhood
Everyone needs someone to hold onto.'

Anon.

Once you begin to like yourself, you become more self-assured. This puts you in control and a self-assured woman who is in control of her life draws other people like a magnet! Now things are beginning to change and you can cancel your membership of the 'If Only' club. Chances are that you may be the same weight as you were before but you have lost the negative attitude of yourself. You feel good inside which shows on the outside – you can believe the very real compliments that you are getting.

Notice that we have not mentioned anything about what to eat (or what not to eat) during this period of positive thinking. This is because, by changing the way you see yourself, you can literally talk yourself out of feeling low, bored, tired, worthless, or lonely. These were probably some of the reasons that sent you heading for food in the first place. You now feel great and you want to go out and socialise, rather than stay at home, feeling miserable, crying into a tub of double chocolate chip ice cream. You may also decide that you don't need to lose weight.

Summing Up

- How you see yourself, and how you think others see you is bound up in your self-esteem. Poor self-esteem can cripple your attitude to life and lead you to take comfort in eating.

- Boost your self-esteem simply by becoming aware of the language you use every day. Make a conscious effort to use positive words, rather than negative ones, in conversation. It is a simple change to make but also fun to notice the subtle changes in yourself, and with other people too!

- Changing your posture, standing 'tall', can have a positive effect on your self-esteem and a knock-on effect on improving your eating habits.

Chapter Eight

Eat Well, Feel Great

A typical comment from habitual dieters is, 'You go on a diet because you don't like your body, but you end up not liking yourself!' Everyone has the potential to be fit, healthy and happy, but a regime of tasteless, low-fat, calorie-counted morsels rarely leaves you with a lip-smacking smile and bounding with energy. Sadly, many people are misinformed about food. Food manufacturers, and government healthy eating advice, have created the illusion that low-fat or low-calorie food is healthy. For the last 30 years, the UK and US governments have championed the 'fat makes you fat' mantra and that a healthy eating plate was one based on loads of the carbohydrate foods and tiny amounts of fatty ones. The food industry responded and supermarket shelves were filled with half-fat cheeses, and low-fat mayo, sausages, biscuits and crisps – so that you can still eat fatty foods, but without the dreaded fat. Skimmed milk (1% fat) was the cornerstone of many weight loss diets, and to even look at a carton of full-fat (a mere 4% fat) was diet suicide. If you take the fat out of foods such as biscuits, chocolate, cakes and ice cream you need to replace it with something. The something was usually sugar, but to make it a lower calorie version, artificial sweeteners were tossed in too. Consequently, most people on a low-fat diet, eat more carbohydrate. Rather than lose weight, in the long term they get fatter. The combination of a high-stress life with a low-fat/high carbohydrate diet has resulted in the obesity epidemic we see today. It would therefore seem obvious that low-fat/high carbohydrate diets don't work contribute to obesity, rather than help to control it. And yet, the advice from the government on how to lose weight has not changed. A popular definition of a fool is 'someone who keeps doing the same thing, but keeps expecting things to be different'. Instead of continuing on this clearly unsuccessful track, the US and UK governments should try something different. Quality foods, chosen for health, should be promoted as these are the ones which your body recognises and can handle. Natural foods such as butter, cream, whole milk, cheese, eggs and meat are far superior to their low-fat 'plastic' counterparts. Good

'Sadly, many people are misinformed about food.'

quality ice cream, made from eggs, cream and sugar is far more satisfying than the low-fat/low-calorie version. Eaten in moderation, the real thing will nourish your body and soul. The same applies to good quality chocolate made from cocoa butter and sugar compared with cheap, poor quality, chocolate which is simply cocoa flavoured margarine. A chocolate cake made with butter, sugar, eggs, flour and milk becomes something to celebrate and enjoy compared with one made with margarine, low-fat milk powder, artificial sweeteners, fillers, emulsifiers and bleached flour.

Here's what to eat

'A chocolate cake made with butter, sugar, eggs, flour and milk becomes something to celebrate and enjoy.'

There is a vast amount of nutrition and food information out there. Making sense of it all can seem a daunting task. However, these few simple principles will transform your food choices, add vitality and help you feel well. They will feed your body a rich variety of natural vitamins, minerals and essential fatty acids which synthetic processed food has lost. The 2011 UK National Diet and Nutrition Survey revealed that the majority of children, teenagers and around half of adult women do not get the basic 'reference nutrient intake' (RNI) amount for iron, zinc, magnesium, potassium, selenium and vitamin D. The mineral content of food is as good as the soil in which it was grown. Eating more naturally grown (preferably using organic farming principles) foods, as close as possible to their natural state, will provide these nutrients. The vitamins and minerals often added back into processed foods may not be in the right form for your body to absorb and use effectively. Adding vitamins A, D, E and K to low-fat foods is often a waste of time, as these fat-soluble vitamins need fat to enable them to be absorbed properly. Remember that low-calorie diets cause your metabolism to slow down – and preserve your fat stores, rather than use them up. Instead, you need to eat more of the right types of foods. These are ones which will boost your metabolism, encourage your fat stores to be used, and prevent large deposits of fat. The right types of foods will also satisfy your appetite, taste good due to their natural flavours, and make you feel good because of their nutrient density. In practice this means eating mainly protein and fatty foods (which will satisfy your appetite), loads of vegetables (to add colour, variety, texture and bulk), and a lot less sugary carbohydrates. Sugars and refined starches will trigger the release of the hormone insulin which will cause excess glucose to be stored as fat.

Protein and fatty foods keep your insulin levels low – which allows the release of fat from your fat stores. Keeping your insulin levels low is a key aspect of effective weight loss. It is important to understanding which foods will do this. The Glycaemic Index (GI) is a measure of the effect of different foods on insulin levels. Over the years, many foods have been tested for their glycaemic effect. Volunteers are asked to eat a particular food, and the change in their blood glucose and insulin levels is measured for the next few hours. Results from these tests have been averaged and GI lists of foods, from all over the world, are available. However, the tests are not always carried out using the same format, and the results will vary. This means that a food on one GI list may have a different value to the same food on another list. These GI lists will give you a rough guide to which foods will promote insulin release, but are certainly not perfect science! Instead, you need to focus on natural fats and protein foods, and limit your intake of carbohydrate to some quality carbohydrate foods.

In summary

- Eat natural fats. If you eat red meat, make sure it is from organic or grass-fed animals. Good quality red meat is expensive, for you and the planet, so enjoy smaller amounts and fill your plate with plenty of vegetables such as cabbage, kale, broccoli, Brussels sprouts, fennel, French beans, mushrooms, red/green/yellow peppers, tomatoes and onions.

- If you eat chicken, make sure it is organic or free range.

- Choose cold pressed vegetable oils such as olive or rapeseed oil – but use these, unheated, in salad dressings or to drizzle over steamed vegetables, rather than frying.

- Serve steamed vegetables tossed in organic butter.

- Buy traditional cheese, the ones that you enjoy, rather than the highly processed half-fat versions.

- Go nuts about nuts. Almonds, Brazils, walnuts, pecans, and unroasted peanuts are a good source of protein and essential fats.

- Enjoy nut butters – peanut butter is the most popular, but tahini (sesame seed paste), almond or cashew butter can be used on wholemeal toast, in soups and with vegetables.

- Read the label and avoid foods with include margarine, hardened fat or hydrogenated fat in the list of ingredients.

After years of eating low-fat versions of foods, the advice to switch to the natural, full fat version, may cause your toes to curl up in horror. Fatty foods may go against your years of unsuccessful calorie-counting routines but they can add so much to your enjoyment of eating, and can help you to lose weight. Whilst studies have shown that low-fat/high carbohydrate eating leads to weight gain, eating natural fats, with good quality protein foods (salmon, mackerel, eggs, cheese, chicken, grass-fed beef or lamb, fermented soya foods such as tofu) and carbohydrate foods as close as possible to their natural state will help you to lose weight.

Choose organic foods. These are certified by the Soil Association in the UK, who regularly visit farms and food manufacturers to check that the organic standards of production are being followed. These do not allow many of the additives (especially colourings and preservatives) which are used in non-organic foods . You won't see any artificial sweeteners or hydrogenated fats on the list of ingredients of an organic food

Enjoy some natural sugars, found in fruits, but avoid processed foods (breakfast cereals, soft drinks, fruit yogurts, poor quality biscuits, cakes, ice-cream), which include any type of sugar (especially high fructose corn syrup) high up in the list of ingredients. These are foods which you may end up eating now and then, sometimes to be sociable, or if you are really desperate, but not those that you would choose to buy on a regular basis. If a processed food has artificial sweeteners, especially aspartame or Sucralose, in the list of ingredients, put it back on the shelf and don't buy it – ever!

What does your new style of eating look like?

Examples of typical meals

Meals should be tasty and satisfying, and a joy to create rather than a chore. Remember, there are no calorie counting or portion sizes to weigh – just focus on putting good quality fat and protein foods together, with loads of vegetables and some fruit.

Breakfast

- Plain, natural full fat yogurt mixed with fresh or frozen berries (strawberries, blueberries, blackcurrants etc.) and chopped walnuts or flaked almonds.
- Chopped fruit (apple, pear, melon, plums, orange or grapefruit) with mixed nuts and seeds (walnuts, Brazils, almonds, hazelnuts, sunflower seeds, pumpkin seeds).
- Omelette – plain or with fillings (ham, chorizo, cheese, red pepper, red onion, tomato, mushroom etc.).
- Scrambled or poached eggs with grilled bacon, tomato, sausage, mushrooms.
- Smoked mackerel with grilled tomatoes.

'Meals should be tasty and satisfying, and a joy to create rather than a chore.'

Main and mini meals

- Chicken or broad bean/chick pea or egg or feta cheese salad with plenty of lettuce, celery, tomatoes, mixed red peppers drizzled with cold pressed olive oil, or an oil/vinegar French dressing.
- Carrot and lentil soup.
- Golden vegetable and mixed bean soup.
- Omelette – plain or with fillings.
- Avocado salad with walnuts, lettuce and olive oil dressing.

- Scrambled egg with smoked salmon.

- Roasted vegetables (cherry tomatoes, red onion, aubergine, red pepper, garlic) on wholemeal toast drizzled with olive oil or grated cheese and grilled.

- Hummus with vegetable sticks (carrot, celery, red pepper, avocado).

- Monkfish with steamed vegetables tossed in butter.

- Roast chicken, lamb, pork or beef with vegetables.

- Poached salmon with salad or steamed vegetables.

- Smoked tofu and bean risotto.

- Venison casserole and roast vegetables.

- Quinoa mixed with roast vegetables, nuts and seeds.

Snacks

- Handful of raw whole almonds and an apple or pear.

- Lump of cheddar cheese and sticks of celery.

- Handful of mixed nuts and seeds.

- Raw almonds and a few squares of dark chocolate.

The most effective way to change is to take a long, hard look at the way you live your life. Then decide to make some small simple changes to your lifestyle including your eating and exercise habits. The rewards are wonderful and they are waiting to be claimed.

Stepping out

Just as a journey of a thousand miles starts with a single step, here are some steps to help you make changes to your eating patterns.

- Write down everything you eat and how you feel at the time. Keep a food diary for a few weeks and examine the patterns that emerge. This will reveal the connection between what you eat, your lifestyle and your emotional state.

- Understand why you are eating – are you emotionally hungry? Do you eat because you are bored, lonely or upset, and use food regularly as a comfort? If so, get back to real hunger. Find other ways to express your emotions. If you eat because you are stressed, then build relaxation into your daily routine. Book a regular massage or reflexology session, listen to soothing music or talk things through with friends, or a trained therapist.

- Focus on yourself and feeling good, rather than the battle of what you can and cannot eat. Weight loss is not about willpower or the calculation of calories in versus calories out.

- Change the way you think about yourself. Your brain is a powerful tool. Use positive thoughts to help boost your self-esteem and guide the way you think and behave.

- Study your eating habits and decide what you need to change. Maybe you already eat good quality foods and it is just the quantity and the portion size of the food you need to change.

- Focus on good quality fats and protein foods, rather than counting calories.

- Believe that your tastes will change. Processed foods are designed to taste good but many are based on the addictive salt, fat and sugar combination. Enjoy discovering the subtle flavours of natural foods. Soon you will find that poor quality foods just taste of salt or that sugary foods are too sickly.

- Small changes = big results. Accept that you are making permanent changes. Most diets are geared towards temporary change. We want to get slimmer for summer or to fit into that little black dress. After that, it is back to our old ways. Once you learn not to diet, but simply to change the way you live, eat and cook, you have taken an important and permanent step. Focus on yourself, and how you want to feel, rather than being ruled by calorie counting or the mistake that low-fat foods are healthy. You will know if you have lost weight – without stepping near any scales. You will feel fantastic, your clothes will fit so well, your skin and muscle tone will improve and above all, you will feel good about yourself.

'Focus on yourself and feeling good, rather than the battle of what you can and cannot eat.'

- Have fun and enjoy life. It is important to build pleasure into a meal. Be experimental and have some fun! If your eating habits have been way out of line, or years of dieting mean that you just don't know how to eat normally anymore, then you might like to set some definite goals and tackle them one at a time.

- Stop dieting and start living. Just think, all that destructive, negative energy spent on feeling guilty and worrying about what you can and cannot eat can be turned into positive power. Who knows what we can achieve if we give up worshipping artificial perfection and start celebrating our own gifts. After all, do we really want to be loved for anything other than our true selves? Find out who you are and celebrate the wonder of your own uniqueness. You need to discover how to express yourself. Find a language that is your own and which doesn't involve food. The answers come from within. If you start to change the way you see yourself and your attitudes towards how you feel and look, you will begin to love yourself. No good longing for that mythical date in the future when things will be different. You are what you are today. Realise that you have control over your life and can do the most fantastic things for you and other people with all that new found positive energy. Use it to stop dieting and start living. After all, success means learning to make the right choices. It is as simple and as straightforward as that.

Decide on the changes you want to make, and do it *now*! There is no better time than now. Take control, makes some changes and bring out the best in yourself. Now is the time to discover your power, and to deal with the core issues which may have blocked your efforts in the past, to forget the fear of food.

Summing Up

- It is time to challenge and change the perceived 'wisdom' that healthy foods are those which are low in calories and/or low in fat.

- Low-fat cheeses, sausage, chocolate, cakes, butter, milk and cream are poor substitutes for the real thing. Some are also full of refined carbohydrate and sugars (to replace the fat).

- Eat real foods. Examples of these are good quality eggs, milk, bacon, sausages, chocolate, vegetables, fruit, bread, beans and butter.

- Real foods will add to the enjoyment of eating, and the pleasures of buying, cooking and sharing food. They will feed your body and soul – which can help to reduce the stress in your life, rather than add to it.

'It is time to challenge and change the perceived 'wisdom' that healthy foods are those which are low in calories and/ or low in fat.'

Help List

Retreat – courses and holidays

Claridge House

Dormans Road, Lingfield, Surrey, RH7 6QH.
www.claridgehouse.co.uk
Tel: 01342 832150
A Quaker centre for healing, rest and renewal. Courses and relaxing breaks including Christmas and New Year retreats.

Cortijo Romero

PO Box 813, Amersham, HP6 9ER.
www.cortijo-romero.co.uk
Offers a variety of self-development courses in Spain. Order a brochure by post or download from the website.

Findhorn Foundation

The Park, Findhorn, Scotland, IV36 3TZ.
www.findhorn.org
Offers a variety of short courses and experience weeks in North Scotland.

Martha Simpson Coaching

Tel: 01651 843492
www.marthasimpsoncoaching.co.uk
Life coaching retreats for women. Small groups, life coaching and time to relax.

Shining Minds Ltd

50/51 Rowes Hill, Horningsham, Wiltshire, BA12 7LQ.
Tel: 0845 6019 577
www.shiningminds.co.uk
Courses and retreats.

Organisations and Associations

Action For Happiness

www.actionforhappiness.org

If you feel stuck in your life and find yourself reaching for food to make you feel better, this site give information, suggestions and resources to add extra elements to your life. Join a happiness project or find out about a new hobby which inspires you and gives you purpose, rather than a short-term fix of the biscuit tin.

Alexander Technique

www.alexandertechnique.com

A qualified teacher will show you how to use your body in a more relaxed and comfortable way. You will learn greater awareness of your body in everyday life, to help you feel better, perform better and prevent back pain and injury. For a list of qualified teachers – The Society of Teachers of Alexander Technique (STAT) – www.statsearch.co.uk.

Byron Katie

Author of Loving What Is.

www.thework.com for worksheets and videos with examples of The Work showing how individuals have turned their lives around.

Chris Fenn

www.chrisfenn.com

Nutrition Consultant

Sign up for my newsletter, or read my nutrition blog on my website.

Eating Disorders

www.eating-disorders.org.uk

Tel: 0845 838 2040

UK help and advice centre.

Emotional Freedom Technique

www.eftuk.com

A technique designed to help with trauma, stress, obsessive and compulsive behaviour. See the website for training courses and list of practitioners.

Food Psychology

Tel: 0141 942 0977
www.thefoodpsychologist.com
Glasgow-based clinic which offers counselling on how to forget calories and low-fat products and eat real foods. Hypnotherapy and addiction therapy also available.

Intuitive Eating

www.intuitiveeating.org
Information and tips on how to make peace with food and give yourself permission to enjoy eating. Learn how to distinguish between emotional and physical hunger.

Neuro Linguistic Programming (NLP)

www.nlpacademy.co.uk
The NLP Academy runs courses and has a list of NLP practitioners in the UK.

Pursuit of Happiness

www.pursuit-of-happiness.org
Learn about the science of happiness. Find out how positive thinking, optimism and the power of gratitude can affect your mood and attitude to life.

Slow Food UK

www.slowfood.org.uk
Part of a global grassroots movement with thousands of members around the world that links the pleasures of foods, produced by traditional methods, with a commitment to community and environment.

Book List

The Artist's Way: A course in discovering and recovering your creative self
By Julia Cameron, Pan, 2011.

Bodies
By Susie Orbach, Profile Books, 2010.

Eat Your Heart Out; Why the food business is bad for the planet and your heart
By Felicity Lawrence, Penguin, 2008.

The End of Overeating; Taking control of our insatiable appetites
By David Kessler, Penguin, 2010.

Everything you Need to Know to Feel Good
By Candace Pert, Hay House UK, 2007.

Feel the Fear and Do It Anyway
By Susan Jeffers, Vermillion, London, 2007.

Food Rules
By Michael Pollan, Penguin, 2010.

Fried; Why You Burn Out and How to Revive
By Joan Borysenko, Hay House UK, 2011.

The Invitation
By Oriah Mountain Dreamer, Element, 2003

Jonathan Livingstone Seagull
By Richard Bach, Element, 2003.

Grow Your Own Drugs
By James Wong, Collins, 2009.

Happiness Now!
By Robert Holden, Hodder & Stoughton, London, 1998.

The Healing Power of EFT and Energy Psychology
By David Feinstein, Donna Eden and Gary Craig, Piatkus Books, 2010.

It's The Thought that Counts; Why Mind Over Matter Really Works
By Dr David Hamilton, Hay House UK, 2008.

Loving What Is; How Four Questions Can Change Your Life
By Byron Katie, Ryder, 2002.

Mind Over Mood; Change How You Feel By Changing the Way You Think
By Christine A Padesky, Guilford Press, 1995.

River Cottage Veg Every Day
By Hugh Fearnley-Whittingstall, Bloomsbury Publishing plc, 2011.

Say No to Diabetes
By Patrick Holford, Piatkus, 2011.

Shift Happens!
By Robert Holden, Hodder & Stoughton, London, 2000.

Trick and Treat; How Healthy Eating is Making Us Ill
By Barry Groves, Hammersmith Press Ltd, 2008.

What To Eat; food that's good for your health, pocket and plate
By Joanna Blythman, Fourth Estate, 2012.

References

Brody, Jane (2011). Still Counting Calories? Your Weight Loss Plan May Be Outdated. New York Times, 18th July 2011.

Green, M.W., Elliman,N.A., & Kretach, M.J. (2005). Weight loss strategies, stress and cognitive function. Supervised versus unsupervised dieting. Phychoneuroendocrinology, 30, 908-918.

Green, M.W. (2001). Dietary restraint and food craving. In M.J.Hetherington (Ed). Food Cravings & Addiction, Leatherhead. Leatherhead Food RA.

Sachs, F.M., Bray, G.A., Carey, V.J. et al (2009). Comparison of Weight Loss Diets with Different compositions of Fat, Protein and Carbohydrate. New England Journal of Medicine, 360; 859-873.

  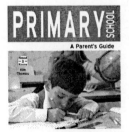  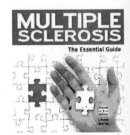